Although we are of the same generation and from the same region of the planet (Zimbabwe, her, South Africa, me), Francisca and I had had such radically different experiences. Her mission seems to be to understand other people and to sow seeds of love and peace, even in the face of generations of injustice. While my path was so much easier, thanks to my white privilege, it takes my breath away to witness her capacity to love and forgive given her life shattering experiences.

—*Jacquie Somerville, writer, speaker, and coach* (*From the forward*)

Francisca Mandeya writes as the ancestor who has returned to earth to wake up those who are asleep. While history has glorified the colonizers' perspective, she speaks for the persecuted. This book offers solutions for dismantling racism, and moving towards liberation for all.

—*June Kaewsith, Your Story Medicine*

SEARCHING FOR *Racial* EQUALITY

AN AFRICAN WOMAN'S URGENT
CALL TO BE ANTIRACIST

FRANCISCA MANDEYA

Copyright © 2022 Francisca Mandeya
Published in Canada by The Transformational Call

All rights reserved. No part of this book may be reproduced, stored, or transmitted by any means—whether auditory, graphic, mechanical, or electronic—without written permission of both the publisher and author, except in the case of brief excerpts used in critical articles and reviews. Unauthorized reproduction of any part of this work is illegal and is punishable by law.

ISBN: 978-1-9992783-4-2 Paperback
ISBN: 978-1-9992783-5-9 eBook
ISBN: 978-19992783-6-6 Hardcover

CONTENTS

Acknowledgments ix
Foreword xiii
Dedication xix
Introduction xxv

1	White Privilege and Black Subjugation 1
2	How Religion is Used to Opiate Africans 19
3	"Black" is Not a Skin Colour 31
4	Letter to Prime Minister Justin Trudeau 43
5	Is There Racism in the Workplace? 53
6	Dear Queen Elizabeth 61
7	Being "Black" in North America 69
8	My "Cousin" Jane Elliot 83
9	To Educate or Indoctrinate: That is the Question 89
10	Swimming is a White Sport 95
11	The Power of a Mother's Teaching 105
12	Creating the Future We Want 111
13	Know Your Roots: From Africa to America 115
14	Toonik Tyme and The Story of the Rainbow 121
15	Had I Known 133
16	Answering the Call 141
17	United Nations Sustainable Development Goals 149

"The very fact that racism degrades both the perpetrator and the victim commands that, if we are true to our commitment to protect human dignity, we fight on until victory is achieved."

—*Nelson Mandela*

ACKNOWLEDGMENTS

To my editor, Rob Okun. Your commitment, support, and effort to ensure I birthed this story safely will forever be cherished. To have an editor like you is a gift, but to have one who also cares about my wellbeing and pays attention to the struggles of pouring out one's heart about such a tough topic, is a blessing. The warmth, love and joy I feel has been invaluable. Throughout this journey, your humility and brilliance always left a smile on my face. Thank you for your way with words and for your guiding questions that helped me find the answers within.

Jacquie Somerville, for the powerful foreword, and for being the unapologetic and beautiful human being you are, I am eternally grateful. Thank you, and Sharla Brown, for your open hearts, humility, tenacity and guidance as my coaches.

Shayla Sima Dube Mabaleka, for being who you are in my life, for getting me, and for the deep conversations and wisdom we have shared, thank you.

June Kaewsith, sage goddess, my SAC Coach thank you for your support and wisdom beyond your years. Coach Shirzad, thank you for all the Positive Intelligence teachings that are sustainably life-changing. My TFT tutors Sally Timmel, Anne

Hope (RIP), Ntombizanele Nyathi, Derrick Naidoo, Priscilla Erasmus, David Kaulemu, Filip Fanchette my father, thank you. TFC USA staff thank you for the trainings.

Joan Wamiti, my young friend, who said to me, "Your voice is needed", I am grateful for the laptop which I used to write this book. Your belief in me propelled me use my voice to do the best I could. Queen Irie, thank you for listening and for cheerleading me along the way!

To my therapist with whom I have journeyed for nearly five years, I am deeply grateful.

And to all those agents of change whose work has broadened my knowledge, thank you. A deep bow of gratitude to Martin Luther King, Jr., Jane Elliot, Ibram Kendi, John Biewen, Prof. Dana Osborne, Paulo Freire, Franz Fanon, Steve Biko, Kimberlé Crenshaw, Mallence Bart Williams, Maya Angelou, Toni Morrison, Rosa Parks, Tata Mandela, Tata Joshua Nkomo.

For the FB race dialogues, Mohammed K Garba, Rebecca Osborne, and Tsitsi Madziwa Nussinov, thank you.

Fellow Iqalummiut, the CanaDiversity cast, thank you for trusting me and showing me that the dream is possible. I appreciate the memories we created and the love I still feel in my heart. Taha Tabish, thank you for both sharing and understanding; I am grateful. Dennis Lambe and Iqaluit RCMP, thank you for your efforts to ensure there is racial equality. Losa Geelaw, thank you for the photo art. Les and Jose Pepito Jr, thank you for the book cover and interior design. Marco Mancinelli thank you for saying yes to using your inspiring photograph, "The Age of Innocence".

Thema McClain thank you for saying yes to me using your powerful photograph: "We do not carry for 9 months." Thank you for the message "God loves you. I literally just woke up, and

I just keep hearing him reminding me to say yes to you." I am grateful for this divine connection and to our answering the call.

Alassua Hanson thank you for being an ally and a part of my story, and for allowing me to use your image.

Jackson and Hudson's parents, Tara and Chris, and Melissa and Jeff, thank you for allowing me to share my son Nicho's story, which includes your children, his brothers. Kuthula and Ivony Matshazi thank you for allowing Sakhile to be a part of my story and to help amplify children's voices. Nadine and Collins thank you for allowing me to include Azriel's story. Kabelo and Febbie Mokoena, thank you for allowing me to include Lesedi's voice in my story. Rowena thank you for allowing me to include your voice. Tracy Lamourie, my ally and friend, thank you for the support and for helping me amplify my voice.

My children, Nomalanga, Zanele & Bobo and Ntando thank you for being my children, for all the experiences we have had—and for the love. My sisters and brothers, Mkoma Tee and Lee, Davie, Julie, Domie- Tina and Jo, my fellow North Americans, thank you for listening and for encouraging me to be smart, brilliant, beautiful, and bodacious. In each of you—in all my siblings—I see my parents. It gives me such joy to know that we love each other no matter what. Tina and Jo, thank you for affirming me, for telling me I am smart and beautiful when I doubted myself. Thank you for our sage dialogues and commitment to being the best versions of ourselves. Mkoma Ange, my big sister thank you. Petronella, I remember you, continue to rest in eternal peace. My uncles and aunties from my mother's side and from my father's side, thank you for being my family.

Friends who have become sisters, Sanele, Dadi and Tafy, Anna-Mary my spiritual daughter and Gladys thank you for our sisterhood and conversations that grow us. Ben, Peter and Malcolm—the rest of our round table members at 5318E, thank you for the conversations.

My husband, David Sothemba Tshuma, Golide, thank you for listening to me and for encouraging me and challenging me through our many deep conversations.

To the Universe, to my Creator, God, thank you for opening up opportunities for me to share my story, and to meet beautiful people in this time of need. Thank you for always making sure my needs are being met. And so it is.

FOREWORD

On the Road to Becoming Antiracist
By Jacquie Somerville

If the choice is you're either racist or antiracist, I grew up racist. Born in the 1960s into the privileged, ruling minority in apartheid South Africa, I benefitted from a system that I knew was wrong, but never protested. As Archbishop Desmond Tutu put it, "If you are neutral in situations of injustice, you have chosen the side of the oppressor." I never thought about it that way until I read Nelson Mandela's 1994 autobiography, *The Long Walk to Freedom*. By that time, South Africa was free, and I was in my late twenties plagued by feelings of remorse. I regretted that I hadn't participated in civil disobedience protests against such blatant injustice.

Francisca Mandeya and I grew up in parallel, yet radically opposing universes. Born of the same generation in the same geographical region of the world, and understanding many of the same colloquialisms, we both knew the feeling of the African sun on our skin, the familiar sight of a clear Southern sky and the sound of pulsing drumbeats, punctuated by the whoops and hollers of African children playing under a dazzling sun.

It was at night that our worlds diverged. The sounds we heard laid bare our dramatically divergent lives. As I slept peacefully and safely in a comfortable bed in a large house lulled by chirping tree frogs and the occasional call of a jackal, Francisca was jarred awake by the terrifying sounds of soldiers kicking in the door of her family's humble dwelling. What she heard were not chirping tree frogs but her mother's screams as she was tortured and terrorized for refusing to reveal the whereabouts of her husband, Francisca's father.

"The fear of potentially losing our mother was tightening my chest; I gagged. In my mind's eye I saw her falling and not being able to get back up. I was crying for Mhamha as the soldiers beat her. She stole helpless glances at us. We could see her agony on her furrowed brow. Still, she refused to say a word about my father."

As I read Francisca's account, my emotions swung wildly from horror to empathy; then, from shame to rage. I realized that the very people who were inflicting such pain and evoking such terror on Francisca's family were the fathers or older brothers of my contemporaries. I grew up on *their* side—the side of the colonizers, the oppressors.

In those days, all white South African men were required to spend a minimum of two years in the military, either after high school or college. What many people do not know, or remember, is that the South African army both supported and fought alongside the Rhodesian army. I remember the stories soldiers told me about when they were called up to the border that separated South

Africa from what was then Rhodesia. I may very well have known some of the men who terrorized Francisca's family.

Looking back, I know I was fortunate to have been raised by parents who taught me that apartheid was wrong. They were kind parents who would not have knowingly associated with anyone who inflicted such cruelty. Yet, still we believed that Nelson Mandela deserved to be in prison. The government-controlled media told us that he would be released if he denounced violence as a method of fighting apartheid. Years later, when I read his book, I finally understood his position and his reasons. He refused to give into the demands of his oppressors. Growing up, though, I wondered why he kept violence on the table.

Perspective is powerful. We are all born with a clean slate and, over time, we learn how to think, how to treat others, how to act, whom to discriminate against, whom to accept. Ultimately, we learn how to *be*. Francisca Mandeya understands this fundamental truth. Consider the beautiful story she tells about her nephew, Nicho, who is of African heritage, and his Caucasian friends, Hudson and Jackson.

> *"Nicho goes to Hudson's and Jackson's homes for sleepovers and they return the visits. They play non-stop when they are together. It is so beautiful to witness untainted love. It is inevitable and sad that there will come a time when someone will "educate" them about their skin colour, which by the way, we all know is not accurate, but that, we are told, is "how it has always been." Would it be too much to ask the world, "Please do not corrupt this love?" Please do not indoctrinate these children with the poison of racism."*

The solution to systemic racism seems so simple. Surely, humans could be more aware of the destructive stories they tell (and perpetuate); they could be more responsible to the future of humanity with the power they wield. "Please do not corrupt this love. Please do not indoctrinate children with the poison of racism." Nelson Mandela said, "No one is born hating another person because of the colour of his skin, or their background, or religion. People must *learn* to hate, and if they can learn to hate, they can be taught to love, for love comes more naturally to the human heart than its opposite."

I was caught between two realities. On the one hand, I comfortably buried my head in the sand, indoctrinated by a monomaniacal broadcasting service (better described as a propaganda service), controlled by a corrupt government. On the other, my soul endlessly questioned discrimination of any kind. "How is it that only Christians go to heaven?" my eight-year-old self mused. "What if I was born to a Hindu family in a remote village in India and was never even exposed to Christianity? How could God possibly send me to Hell for something that wasn't my fault?" I was baffled. If there was a God, surely He or She wasn't cruel or discriminatory. There was no answer satisfactory to me, so I began to reject the religion of my birth.

Around the same time, and from a privileged vantage point sitting on my English saddle atop my perfect little pony, I'd witness men dressed in rags cutting the sugar cane on the corporate sugar estate I grew up on. Exhausted, they would walk "home" to a mud hut and a meagre meal cooked over an open fire. "Why are the cane-cutters so poor?" I asked. "Why are their children not allowed to come to my school?" I asked. Neither my parents, nor any other adults, offered any satisfactory answers.

As a child, I did not know what to do about any of these

things that I innately knew were so very wrong. I was baffled why God would create a world in which some people were "the chosen ones" and others were "condemned" to be "lesser beings". As Francisca so movingly writes, "The heartache of being African and knowing we are at the bottom rung of the race ladder, and therefore not viewed as equals by most of the world, was real."

In *Searching for Racial Equality,* Francisca answers questions that have plagued me for decades, among them: What are the origins of racism? How, and why, did the colonizers do what they did? Why are so many people driven to perpetuate racial divisions and stereotypes? These questions—and many others—must be wrestled with. After all, without understanding each other's perspective, we can never achieve peace.

If I could wave a magic wand, I would have everyone read Francisca's account of her daughter's experience at a swim meet in Zimbabwe. The chapter title says it all: "Swimming is a White Sport." My skin was covered with goose bumps as I read this deeply personal story about an angry white woman who referred to Francisca's daughter as "that Black thing." Why? Because she was victorious over her white daughter in a "white sport." With that one phrase, she killed the confidence and spirit of a child who had overcome hydrophobia to become an amazing swimmer—*and* she planted the seeds of racism in her own daughter's heart.

Whoa… there it is—the power of an authority figure's words! That's it in a nutshell. To stop this horrifying behaviour, we have to stand up to such people. We must never miss an opportunity to challenge hate speech. We will never stop racism if we tolerate it, even a little bit. We can no longer remain silent as it continues all around us in both overt and subtle ways. It will require a radical rewiring of our brains, and emotional surgery to open our hearts.

Only then will we be able, possibly, to proclaim that we are on the road to becoming antiracist.

In this extraordinary and urgently important book, Francisca Mandeya challenges us to consider a new way of being: "Unless we accept the undeniable truth that we are one human race, and we remove all blame, guilt, shame, *and* commit to healing ourselves and to never again allowing a system of dominants and subordinates… there will be no peace…."

Despite all the abuse and indignities she and her family suffered, her heart remained open. It still does. Begin with ourselves, she implores us. Forgive ourselves. Forgive others. Choose love over fear. If she can, we can, too.

Although we are of the same generation and from the same region of the planet (Zimbabwe, her; South Africa, me), Francisca and I had had such radically different experiences. Her mission seems to be to understand other people and to sow seeds of love and peace, even in the face of generations of injustice. While my path was so much easier, thanks to my white privilege, it takes my breath away to witness her capacity to love and forgive given her life shattering experiences.

Knowing how Francisca chooses to live her life gives me hope for our fragile world. I feel we are kindred spirits. As she likes to point out, none of us are either "black" or "white"—we're a shade without a label—one with the Divine. Descended from a common ancestor in Africa, we are One.

Los Angeles, California
October, 2021

A writer, speaker, and coach, Jacquie Somerville travels the world inspiring women and girls to live life with passion and purpose.

DEDICATION

To the Light that is my Mother and
the Fire that is my Father

I dedicate this book to my forever young parents, my mother, Lucia Chavanga-Mandeya, and father, Ignatius Mandeya, whom I watched being abused, beaten and tortured—not once, not twice, not thrice—but countless times in my first decade on this earth. Their so-called crime? Resisting the Rhodesian British-backed soldiers who fought against Zimbabwe's independence.

Thank you for being my parents. Thank you for teaching my siblings and me resilience, forgiveness, love, kindness, sacrifice, humility, hard work, and charity. Thank you for affirming me and allowing me to be fearless and to speak my mind, even as a toddler. The full realization of what I witnessed you go through, enduring all that pain, torture and suffering in your youth while raising us. It hit me after you were gone. I salute your resilience, your love.

Despite all the cruelty you endured you were never cruel. You embraced many, even though some of them "embraced you back" while holding knives with which they stabbed you in betrayal, before, during and after our country's liberation struggle. You always forgave them.

Thank you for teaching us the importance of education and hard work. Thank you for being caring to our community and teaching us to treat each person with respect. We have not forgotten the many new relatives you gave us despite having no official blood relationship with them. We see you in them and often wonder what you might have looked like in old age. Your love for them makes us see you in them. It is strange, but when we put flowers on your graves we see those remaining relatives; the connection is powerful and enduring.

Thank you for modeling how to do business with kindness as you set the prices in your general store with the community in mind. Because you cared about them, you chose to take less profit and leave customers with some money in their pockets.

You were punished for your sacrifice and love of our country, paying heavily for supporting the comrades in our country's liberation struggle. You never sought praise for what you did; you never sought special recognition. I have made a point of making sure your grandchildren heard the stories of your struggles with racial discrimination, the pain I witnessed you endure and how you refused to let it poison your loving, generous, kind souls. You rose from the ashes to revive Mandeya store in Wedza Goto after the Rhodesian government destroyed it.

I am grateful to God for being your child and I have faith that you are resting in eternal peace. I was lucky to have you both raising me. As I reviewed the arc of your lives, for a long time I struggled with grief, feeling the pain you felt and questioning why your lives had to be the way they were. I am consoled by the impact you left; I no longer question your journeys. Now at 51, an age by which you were both already gone, I memorialize you and hope I can do half the things you did for others. I write this book to honour and celebrate you. I also remember all the parents who suffered as you did and those who died fighting to free our country from colonial rule.

Every family has its story. To the Light, that is my mother and to the Fire that is my Father, to my descendants, born of this pedigree, may the family legacy of love never die. Baba, I know that when you visit me in my dreams every problem and challenge goes away. Mhamha, while you don't visit as often, I feel your light and peace. My heroes, my angels—until we meet again.

I Am the Light

I am the light that strives to drive out
The darkness in me. I choose to be
Positive and to love unconditionally,
Beginning with myself.

The thing called freedom
The thing called freedom
Is just a dream
The thing called freedom
The thing called freedom
Is but my dream

Since time immemorial we have been fighting for freedom
Freedom from poverty in all its kinds
Freedom from repression of the human mind
Freedom from racism in all its colours

Lend me wings
Wings of freedom
I wanna fly away
To the land of the free

Walk me, walk me
Fly me, fly me
Carry me, carry me
Take me, Take me

Tata Mandela
Walk me, walk me
Fly me, fly me
Carry me, carry me
Take me, Take me

Joshua Nkomo
Walk me, walk me
Fly me, fly me
Carry me, carry me
Take me, Take me

Rosa Parks
Walk me, walk me
Fly me, fly me
Carry me, carry me
Take me, Take me

Martin Luther King
I have a dream....

The thing called freedom
The thing called freedom
Is just a dream
The thing called freedom
The thing called freedom
Is but my dream

Lend me wings
Wings of freedom
I wanna fly away
To the land of the free

There is a culture
Of silence
Of arrogance
And violence
I won't dance to this tune!

—Francisca Mandeya, 2008

INTRODUCTION

I AM! My Identity, My Fundamental Human Right

I am Francisca Ndaiziweyi Mandeya. I was born on March 7, 1970, during the violent liberation struggle between indigenous Zimbabweans and the British. I arrived on this earth just five days after the republic of Rhodesia was established. My parents, Ignatius (Fire), and Lucia (Light), were Manyika from Manicaland. They chose to migrate to Mashonaland East and live with the Zezuru, eking out a living as rural business people. It is in St. Anne's Goto cemetery in Mashonaland East that they lie, side by side in eternal peace.

I am rooted in my culture and at peace with my ancestors. I use my culture to heal and free myself—and others—from the chains of mental slavery. Racism is a thief that stole the voice of my ancestors by demonizing their culture, their gods, and the core of who they were. Racism is a killer, an adulterer who has grossly violated the rights of my people.

I am Catholic because my parents were Catholic. As required, I was baptized into Christianity before I could speak. History taught me that the white man, the colonizer, came with a bible in one hand and a gun in the other. The uncomfortable truth is that Christianity is shrouded in racism. How could my voice be mine when I had to assume an identity imposed on my parents, albeit accepted amid confusion and straddling between two belief systems—one imposed by outside proselytizers; the other the native spiritual expressions of my people? Under such conditions, how could my consciousness be mine? How could my mind be at rest?

I am African. I am proud to be Bantu and to still subscribe to the philosophy and values of Ubuntu, where human life comes first, before wealth and all else. I am proud to come from a place where the majority of people are loving and kind, people who find happiness in the "small things."

I am Zimbabwean. Almost at the soles of Africa's feet is a country shaped like a teapot without a handle, Zimbabwe and she is endowed with rich soil and mineral wealth. She boasts of the mighty Mosio oa Tunya (the smoke that thunders), blandly renamed as Victoria Falls by the British after David Livingstone "discovered" them.

Zimbabwe is also known for the Great Zimbabwe ruins (the capitol of the Queen of Sheba, according to legend); the beautiful Eastern Highlands; Mutarazi and Nyangombe Falls; and Hwange National Game Park, among many other breathtaking tourist attractions.

I am told that I might not be Zimbabwean but in fact Mozambican! Word of mouth has long suggested that before colonialists came, Rusape was part of Mozambique. What does it matter—African, Zimbabwean or Mozambican? They are all colonial identities. There were no boundaries before the scramble for Africa. African people freely moved up and down the continent. Accordingly, identity by country was nonexistent.

So, who am I? My people were just Bantu, *vanhu* in my language, simply meaning "people." They were Bantu who lived according to the values of Ubuntu, the philosophy that "I am because you are." I am comfortable in the brown skin that I did not choose to be born in. I prefer being called African rather than a colour-related identity. I am like dark chocolate. I come from a country where some of its colonial scars can be found on the cheekbones of women in their sixties, seventies, and eighties, women who were burnt by hydroquinone as they lightened and whitened their skin to look more like their colonial masters. When I investigated my ancestry, I learnt I am 49 percent southern Bantu; 48 percent Cameroon, Congo and western Bantu, and three percent eastern Bantu.

I am a Gwenyambira, a mbira player. The mbira is a therapeutic, traditional Zimbabwean instrument more than a thousand years old, a treasure from our ancestors. (Also sometimes referred to as an African thumb "piano." (The kalimba is a smaller, modern version of the mbira.) I have witnessed the power of music as a vehicle for social change.

I am a Mother, a life giver. I believe that the gift of giving life is sacred. The right to life must be respected and every child no matter who they are born to, matters. I am a proud mother. I feel privileged to know the power of love—my body housed three human beings for 27 months before they entered this world! Motherhood taught me to love at another level, to serve and not to think twice about who comes first in my life. Motherhood is leadership and, as Spiderman reminds us, "With leadership comes great responsibility." I long for my children to enjoy lives of equality and freedom and, as I shared in my first book, *Mother Behold Thy Son*, to choose love.

I am the wife of Tshuma Golide, the man who made me eat my words about not dating African men. I am grateful for the gift of love and friendship.

I am a global citizen.

I traversed the globe from the blazing Zimbabwean sun to the frigid Canadian Arctic. I feel privileged to be on the land of the Inuit where I have felt safe (for the most part) and have come full circle. I have friends, acquaintances, sisters and brothers, not born of my parents; they may have come from different cultures and have different physical appearances than me. Still, we have forged healthy relationships together.

I am human.

I am just like you. My true identity dwells within me, as yours lives within you. You cannot tell who I am by looking at my skin. My humanity is not defined by my geography, my demography, my biography or choreography. It is what is in my heart that makes me human. What is in your heart makes you the same. I am what is in my heart; not my skin, just as you are what is in your heart, and not your skin. I am just like you.

Ubuntu: I am because you are; you are because I am. Covid-19 has reinforced the stark truth that life is not about the "I"; it is about the "we"—it is about us. We are all connected. We are interdependent. We are one.

I am the daughter of I AM.

I am created in the image of I AM, the all-powerful, the Almighty. The one who is forever present and never absent. I am fearfully and wonderfully made, awesomely melanated and marinated by the African sun. I am fully and completely deserving of equal opportunities like any other human being. I am a master of my own life. I am not a victim. I am a victor. I have been spared many times. I cannot say I am alive because I am clever. I know that God has preserved my life.

At times I chuckle and say, "I am a moving political statement." Identity politics is full of lies. White lies and Black lies! I refuse to be contained, packaged, sealed up in a box. I refuse to be saddened by the current state of racial inequality— even as I must acknowledge my anger!—and declare my equality with any other human being born of woman. *I* get to define my identity.

I am a future ancestor, creating the future I want to see. I choose to make my ancestors proud by listening to their whispers, imploring me to "Wake up, wise up, rise up, speak up! My unequivocal answer? "I will!"

CHAPTER ONE

White Privilege and Black Subjugation

"*Mandeya, vhura!*" a thunderous knock on our door, followed by a violent kick and growling voice commanding my father to open it. It was past midnight on that fateful night in October, 1975. I have a vivid memory of my mother coming out of the bedroom in a thin, pink nightgown. She must have been breastfeeding my two-week-old little sister, Juliet Chipo Chedenga Chamapihwa. She stood behind the dining room door, hesitating. Then, before she could decide what to do, a white Rhodesian soldier kicked it open with such force it hit my mother in the head. She staggered back, trying to maintain her balance.

Our family was supporting the liberation fighters, the comrades, who were resisting Ian Smith's white supremacist, pro-colonialist Rhodesian government which vehemently opposed handing over power to Black rulers.

My father was being accused of not only supporting the

communist-backed liberation fighters financially and with moral support, but also knowing where their bases were. The same two Rhodesian army officers, Bristol and Stewart, regularly tortured my father, demanding he tell them where they could find the comrades. Sometimes they showed up with other soldiers; sometimes, sadly, Black soldiers were among them.

"Where is your husband?" Bristol barked, lifting the butt of his gun threateningly, impatiently waiting for a response. "He is not here," Mhamha quietly answered. Bristol struck her in the face with the butt of his gun. Reeling, she hit her head on the wall. The force of the blow took her down.

"Jesu," she moaned. When she heard the pounding on the door, my mother commanded my father to hide, preferring to take the officers' blows to seeing her husband killed on the spot. If I close my eyes I can still hear her groaning.

My two older sisters, Tendai, nine, and Elizabeth, seven, and I were sleeping on the floor of our what we called our "dining room." Our house had three rooms. There was a kitchen with a huge Dover stove and a standby gas stove, then the dining room in the middle, and our parents' bedroom at the end. The store that my father built with his own hands was a stone's throw away from our house. The piece of land that separated the two buildings is where we used to spread a reed mat and enjoy our heavy breakfast on Saturdays. It was also our playground and sun basking spot. Having a "heavy" breakfast was a reward after a week of none of us having a proper breakfast during the week as the family rushed to work or school. While I don't remember what day the soldiers came, I took comfort knowing I would have heavy breakfast soon.

Imagine yourself as a little child in dreamland, dreaming of eating great food and then, maybe chasing butterflies. Now, imagine waking up to the reality of your mother being brutalized. It was horrific to witness. I did not understand why grown men would come not only to interrupt my sleep, but to harm my mother. I hated them.

We had been told to always run and hide under the bed or sofa when we heard the sound of the Rhodesian soldiers' vehicles. That night there was nowhere to hide. We were sleeping on the floor and the soldiers had pounced, unannounced! "Bury your heads in those blankets and go to sleep now!" a soldier barked. Trembling, we did as we were told.

"What will happen to our Mhamha?" I thought, my heart racing. It felt like it would jump out of my chest as it slammed against my breastbone. Even at five, my head and heart knew that my mother could die. I knew even then that guns kill. I knew violence. Childhood innocence is a luxury reserved for privileged, cushioned children. I knew they were hurting my mother; I was hurting, too. So were my sisters. We all knew none of us could say a word as long as the soldiers were there. We could not cry. I could not dare go out to pass urine, so I wet the blankets, something I had last done when I was three.

Just then my chronic cough punctured the silence. It was a terrible cough that once it began regularly unsettled the whole family. I had stayed under the covers as instructed. Unfortunately, I just could not breathe easily. Pain shot through my chest. As I coughed violently, my sisters elbowed me to be quiet but I could not control the cough. I cried out, instinctively throwing off the blankets, gasping for air. Now all of us could see what was going on because we shared the blankets and I was in the middle. I knew the pain of knowing what the soldiers could potentially do; it was killing me. My chest felt like it was in a vice and I could taste the fear that we might lose our mother. I gagged. In my mind's eye I saw her falling and not being able to get back up.

I was crying for Mhamha as the soldiers beat her. She stole helpless glances at us. We could see her agony on her furrowed brow. Still, she refused to say a word about my father. Such fierce love for him! My mother did not think twice about it. I had seen it many times when the soldiers harassed her for information. She would always protect my father. I had seen it in the many stunts she pulled to fool the soldiers, claiming she had a toothache and tying a scarf around both cheeks, or miming that her voice was gone; that she was too hoarse to talk. All to protect her man—my father.

I saw it on the Christmas, Easter and birthday cards she penned to him over the years. They were all written in her well-formed, cursive handwriting. I probably wasn't supposed to read my father's cards, but I always did with both a smile and a bit of embarrassment. Mother was very expressive. "My beloved husband Ignatius," she would start, "your loving wife Lucia," she would sign off. In between she would weave sentences replete with heartfelt words of love and gratitude.

Political prisoners and war orphans

They say when you truly love someone, you can die for your loved one. Mhamha taught that well. In war, in peace, and until death, she loved my father.

Between sobs and coughs, I saw my father returning. He cast a glance at us and held up two fists in a sign of defiance and solidarity. He was signalling for us to be strong before turning himself in. My heart sank. They were going to beat Baba again as they had done before. They had already beaten Mhamha. Baba asked them to leave her alone. I am sure it took just a few minutes for Baba to come out, but for me it seemed like an eternity. I desperately wanted it to end. I said a little prayer for the soldiers to just go.

As if possessed by a violent spirit, the white soldier struck my father with his gun on the forehead and he went down hard. As he staggered to stand, Bristol slapped him and threw him against the wall, pinning him there. He laughed, spat at him, and promised him death. My heart was now in my throat. I don't know what my sisters were doing. I felt like standing up and screaming at them: "Stop hurting my parents!!!" They all looked like monsters. They threatened Baba. "We're going to kill you, but first don't lie to us. Mandeya, *Upi lo gandanga*? (Where are the comrades?)" the soldiers demanded. They spoke Chilapalapa, a language they used for people who did not understand English. He said it in a mocking way.

Another soldier chimed in, "Oh, right, just like your wife didn't know where you were?" Bristol interjected, "You are going to tell us where they are! We have not even started with you." My mother stood by, but she was playing with her fingers as if she was doing the Rosary. Maybe she was. My breathing finally normalized when they stopped beating Baba.

The soldiers dragged him to the Land Rover they had parked outside, and bundled him into the back. My mother followed to see what would happen next.

"You too," Bristol snarled, pointing at my mother.

"I have a baby, and my other children need me," she appealed.

Bristol's cold stare and furrowed brow was enough of a response. He flared his nostrils as if the pit latrine a few metres away was offending him and snapped, "Go get your monkey and follow your husband. You are always lying that he is not home. Today we found him right here! What do you have to say for yourself?"

My mother quietly went back into the bedroom where my year-and-a-half-year-old baby sister, Tina, and my three-year-old brother, David, were asleep. Mhamha emerged with proper clothes on, carrying my little sister and her nappy bag.

It was like a funeral as we heard them go. Without the soldiers to shut us up, we cried our hearts out as we searched each other's faces for signs of strength. We had no answers about when or if our parents would come back home. As soon as I tried to sleep, the soldiers' bright pink, then angry red faces kept haunting me as I imagined what they were doing to my parents. The Queen gave them permission to do what they were doing to my parents.

It all started with Rhodes

When I was 10, our fourth-grade textbook had my classmates and me in stitches. We had read a passage describing Cecil Rhodes (credited with "discovering" our land) waking his friends up in the middle of the night to ask them if they agreed with him that the British were the finest race on earth. Despite having witnessed British brutality, my friends and I laughed convulsively, as did our teacher.(The colonies Rhodes "founded", Southern and Northern Rhodesia, were renamed Zambia in 1964, and Zimbabwe in 1980).

The way the book was written obscured and diluted the impact of Rhodes' white supremacy. We laughed it off. Decades later, when I came to the Canadian North and met Inuit who regularly confront racism—and readily talk about historical injustices—I knew I was in a place, and with a people, where I had permission to speak my truth without fearing ridicule.

Some people have suggested that there are times that it's better for the colonizer to come back because at least under colonial rule, "We lived a better life in terms of having most of our basic needs satisfied." Now I realize how education can present serious issues in persuasive ways aimed at "domesticating" us to accept the status quo. It makes us feel smart when we rationalize such events. We stop people from questioning and dealing with racial injustice because we think we know it all.

The underacknowledged truth about those books is that they all were written by white people from a white supremacist viewpoint. They determined the curriculum. If my father and mother had published those books, we would not have laughed; I know we would have cried.

In my pursuit of liberation, I have come to realize that education is not neutral. I first learnt this from the writings of radical educator Paulo Freire (author of the *Pedagogy of The Oppressed* and *Education for Critical Consciousness*). He believed that education either liberates us—and helps us to solve problems—or it domesticates us to the status quo. If we are experiencing injustice we need to question the education we have received. Has it liberated us? If not, why not?

I found that when I began asking myself those questions I started being curious about Dr. David Livingstone, the Scottish missionary and explorer who sought to bring Christianity and "civilization" to Africa. I laughed out loud recalling how even our child's plays had been infiltrated by white supremacist propaganda. Consider this ditty my playmates and I would thoughtlessly chant: "Christopher Columbus was a great man; he went to

America in a saucepan. He went to Umtali, Umtali andie oooverr. Two little sausages in a saucepan, one went plop, and another went bye."

I learnt that Columbus—who generations have been taught had "discovered" the land that became the US—was *not* a great man. He was a white supremacist whose only "discovery" was that he had arrived on land that had been long inhabited by Native Americans. I had to acknowledge to myself that I had grown up reciting children's rhymes that sang the praises of white supremacists.

White people wielded both economic and political power and dictated where Blacks could and could not go. In urban areas, no Blacks were allowed in the central business district. This was not peculiar to my country. All countries in the region created a similar hierarchy. Growing up, I remember my aunt using the terms "colour bar" and "racial discrimination." Not that I knew what those terms meant then. In South Africa it would be called apartheid. White people were at the top rung of the race ladder; then Asians; then coloureds; and finally brown-skinned Africans—erroneously referred to as "Blacks."

Such classifications came with privilege for those at the top rung and none for those of us teetering precariously on the bottom of the ladder. So, it had been intentional, by design, that my parents were subjugated through torture and incarceration and lost all their wealth to the British. White supremacists saw nothing wrong with such dehumanization. My parents were never meant to be successful, to thrive; they certainly were never meant to support the liberation struggle. Blacks were supposed to limit their participation in society to working for white supremacists, abetting them as they accumulated economic wealth and consolidated political power. They created laws that served them. To this day, I have wondered why some former Rhodesians are so unapologetic about the economic disparities we Africans lived under; many still are rude when talking to some of us. They truly believed, like Cecil Rhodes and Ian Smith (and all those who ruled us in between), that whites were the "finest" race, and they could kill, torture, maim and still be described as "gentlemen." On the other hand, true freedom fighters, those who sought our liberation, were labeled as "terrorists."

White men raped Black women as they pleased, a reality that has never been openly confronted by Zimbabweans because the culture of silence around some details of the liberation struggle prevails. The war was bloody, cruel, barbaric and inhumane, justified as a necessary evil to "civilize" us. I bore witness of this process of "civilizing."

I often wondered why some Africans ended up working for the Rhodesian army. Was it a part of their being "civilized"? I remember hearing the term "call up"—that at age 18 a lot of Africans were "called up" to work for the army. Called up was no doubt a euphemism for being forced into the army. I have been told that Rhodesian officials enticed young recruits with promises of money and a better life. Many were seduced by the so-called glamour surrounding battle.

The fog of war distorts the truth, purporting to only show veterans decorated with medals. My experience of war does not fool me; I do not buy into the belief that war is the best "conflict resolution" tool in this world. In my experience, war produces trauma and untold suffering for so many. Only the well-to-do benefit, thinking only about their bottom line.

My parents endured multiple abuses: physical, psychological, emotional; like all of their brother and sister survivors, they were told to "let bygones be bygones." Remarkably, they did. Could they really, and still be able to rebuild their lives?

They reminded me of a plant called mufandichimuka, literally meaning, "I die and then resurrect." It thrives on hilly or rocky areas. It can appear dry and lifeless but when put in water, it comes back to life; its leaves quickly turn from brown to green. Like the mufandichimuka plant, resilience was in my parents' genes. They were born to bounce back.

The Return

Shouts and whoops filled the air as I saw two figures, a man and woman, approaching our compound. The woman was holding a baby about three months old. I was not the only one yelling. It must be them! Who else would be crossing into our backyard? Even though Mother looked terrible, her eyes sad and distant, still the corners of her mouth turned up in her signature toothless grin. Her smile was coming back! My father also looked dreadful. He was unusually quiet; the fire that burned in him nearly extinguished. Still, he also smiled. And, with their smiles embers of hope flickered stronger in me. He was fine; or at least I believed in my heart that he would be. I was the girl who looked like her daddy. He was my hero and he was back, albeit not looking heroic. But he was back! She was back! Our parents were home! We had gotten used to the emptiness of being war orphans, but their surprise return made us whole again.

Their hair was uncombed and dirty. Their gaunt, battered bodies were evidence of the suffering they had endured. Even though they almost looked like strangers we knew it was them!

Squealing with excitement, we ran to welcome them. My mother immediately put her hand like a police officer stopping traffic. *They didn't want us anymore?* My little five-year-old heart tugged at me as I looked from one to the other. Then she said, "Inda ne tsikidzi"! We are covered with lice and bed bugs. We need to be clean first."

My baby sister, Juliet Chipo Chedenga Chamapihwa, was so thin you might have thought that even if you hugged her gently she would break. Her eyes were huge and sunken, and her hair was greasy. Despite the torture they had endured while imprisoned, my mother's humour never left her. My parents and sister had lived in "four in one" confinement barracks where the kitchen, dining room, bedroom and toilet where all in one room. Mhamha told us that she named my sister Tiny because she was not growing well; noticeably malnourished and sickly. She suffered an untreated ear infection while in prison and Mhamha feared that she had developed hearing problems.

If tears had been harvested that day we would have collected bushels. My siblings and I cried with joy. They were back. They did not die. To be honest, in my brain—and heart—they had been gone for a long time. I still don't know how long they'd been jailed but it was long enough for my baby sister to come out malnourished.

Mhamha and Baba cut each other's hair as well as Tiny's. After they bathed, they burnt the clothes they had been wearing. Baba shaved his beard that had grown long like an Apostolic sect member. Soon, these ex-prisoners looked less ghastly, more relaxed and happier. Our status as orphans was over—for now. We were grateful.

I do not remember who cooked, but we all sat outside on the

reed mat to feast on good food. My mother, a gifted storyteller, moved us to tears with her tales. That day we sang songs of joy. Music always made our family happy. Mhamha could really sing! A long time after my mother had died, my cousin Rose disclosed that the Rhodesian Broadcast Corporation had aired Mhamha's and her friend's performance of a song that had won a music competition. Mhamha never told the story, but judging from her vocal range I was not surprised. That day, on the reed mat, we sang church and fun songs. Singing brought us joy, no matter what was happening.

> *We are here to sing about letters*
> *M stands for Mandeya G stands for girls E stands for ever and S stands for smiling*
> *M stands for Mandeya B stands for boys E stands for ever and S stands for smiling*
> *M stands for Mandeya F stands for Family E stands for ever and S stands for smiling.*

1978: The Lost Future

Child development experts say the most crucial time in a child's development are the formative years, from birth to eight. I have often wondered how many children's formative years have been coloured with violence and instability. How that must impact their futures? If you have had such an experience, I want you to know you are not alone.

A childhood memory: One minute, a shiny toy was in the hands of two seven-year-olds. Fascinated by its luminous exterior, and both eager to peek inside, they fought for it, one pulling on one end and one on the other. Then, *BOOM!* The flash of light could be seen from our grade 1 and 2 block at St. Anne's Goto primary school. The marshlands just outside the schoolyard, less than a thousand metres away, drank the blood of one of the children, Kay. Tee remained with the pin in his hand, shell-shocked that a toy could be so cruel to kill his best friend, just like that.

The two boys had left their newfound toy carefully hidden in the thick grass to play with during recess. Our teacher ran to investigate. When he returned we learnt that we were never going to see Kay again. Kay was just a heap of flesh and blood in an unrecognizable, tattered school uniform. I was not a direct witness to the accident, but I will never forget how my mind wanted to go over the details of how it happened, what it looked like, and why in heaven's sake Kay had to die. He was the smartest boy in grade one.

The unexploded grenade must have come from an exchange between the soldiers who had camped at our homestead and the comrades suspected of being in the marshland. I was holding my intestines in my hands that night. Which sound did we not hear? Big bombs, small bombs, big guns, small guns. "That one is an AK 47, that one was is a NATO, that one is a grenade." Meanwhile my sisters and cousins were busy naming the guns while I was expelling personal bombs, farting myself to comfort. I was a nervous wreck.

My cousin Angie was 16; my elder sisters, Tendai and Elizabeth, were 12 and 10 respectively. We had moved from sleeping on the floor of our three-room house to the floor of the store that my father built with his own hands. I guess our parents thought it was safer there and also because our cousin Angela had come to stay with us. That night my prayer to God to save us and our parents had worked.

1979: Silence the Children, The War Collaborators

"Don't shoot them! Shoot me instead," Mhamha begged, pleading with the soldiers to spare our lives. A gun was pressed between my eyes and two other guns were pointed, one at my little brother David's head and one at my cousin Petronella's head. Mhamha had come flying out of the store when she had seen the soldiers. At the corner of our garden she saw us being held at gunpoint. She put her hands in the air, pleading, "Don't shoot! They are just children! You can shoot me."

Had Mhamha not sensed that we were in trouble, we would have been shot dead that day. I can still smell the acrid odor of the gun against my head. Our "offence" was monkeying around in the trees that bordered a little rivulet that flowed behind the cattle and goat pens, less than a hundred metres from our homestead. The moment we heard the soldiers were on their way to our home we had climbed down the Mukute tree and ran home as fast as we could.

The soldiers claimed we deserved to die because we were war collaborators, relaying messages from our parents to the comrades. The war collaborators were called *Chimbwido* if female and *Mujibha* if male. What was ridiculous was that I was 9, my brother, 7 and my cousin Petronella, 10. We later learnt that they had seen us through their binoculars as we were hurriedly climbing down the big Mukute tree we liked playing in. We always ran to safety when we saw or heard their vehicles approaching. On that day though, they caught us! Thank God for our loving, intuitive, brave and protective mother and aunt.

That year, 1979, was the most violent and traumatic of our young lives—(as it was for many, even though not everyone in the community experienced the level of violence my parents did). They had received warnings that the soldiers were going to kill our whole family. Thank God for our cousin Angela. One of the African soldiers liked her, and he let the cat out of the bag so she was able to warn us!

Under the pretext of attending our uncle CD's wedding in Umtali (now called Mutare), we were able to escape. After the wedding, we never returned home. We migrated to Marandellas (now Marondera) to live with Uncle DX at Bernard Mizeki College. Mhamha and Baba lived in the ghetto in Dombotombo with the siblings Tina, Julie and Domie who were not attending school. Calculating back, I believe Mhamha was carrying her eighth child, our last-born, Jo.

Even though we experienced violence, displacement and their related traumas, we were not a sad family. We had many occasions to celebrate, including weddings, birthdays, births, and academic excellence. We cherished the simple things in life like playing outside, horseplay, pada, water, sweetie, dunhu, dollhouse, aeroplane, tsoro and tree climbing which, more often than not, got me, my brother and cousins into trouble.

1980: Independence!

When I turned 10 in 1980, our country achieved independence from British rule. We returned home. My parents repaired the holes in the building where the soldiers had shot it up to vent their anger when they discovered an empty home. They were angry that we had escaped. My parents restocked the shelves of their general store, having secured a bank loan, thanks to Uncles DX and CD, teaming up to provide collateral. GT Tselentis, a Greek businessman who became my father's friend, helped with short-term credit. Uncle DX told us my parents paid back the loan in full in no time. Mandeyas bounce back!

When I think back to this time in my life, I am better able to understand the hypervigilance and victimhood that ruled me for decades. White supremacy and Black subjugation were certainly a part of it. As an adult trauma survivor, I know I have been hijacked by anger, frustration, anxiety, and constant worry. I have questioned my existence, asking God, "Why?" Why did You create us differently? Why are we the "unwanted species?"

While I cannot erase these horrible childhood memories, I have learnt to channel negative emotions toward positive outcomes. I understand that my life's story remains key to finding my purposes. I write and play mbira; I sing and speak out. I continue my lifelong desire to free myself—and I am still learning. I refuse to let my past dictate my future. My past will not imprison me!

I declare that the voice of children must be heard. Their cries must not be silenced. Adults must think of their future when they make decisions. I continue to do everything necessary to not remain hijacked by my past. I cannot change my past, but I can surely change my "now"—and my future. I have committed to the continuous healing of the self. Sharing my story is part of my healing.

As Shirzad Chamine, once chair of the largest coach-training organization in the world says, "There is a gift and opportunity in every outcome and circumstance." I choose to see what happened in the first decade my life as offering me the gift of inspiration. My story is no longer just for me. Yes, I watched my parents being treated like they didn't matter; their youth stolen, stifled in their prime by a repressive system of racial discrimination. Stripped of their wealth and displaced from their home, still they bounced back. They revived their business. They were resilient. *We* are resilient. *We* can bounce back no matter how much damage is done. We are designed to bounce back!

CHAPTER TWO

How Religion is Used to Opiate Africans

Evangelize the niggers so that they stay forever in submission to the White colonialists, so they never revolt against the restraints they are undergoing. Recite every day, "Happy are those who are weeping because the kingdom of God is for them."

—King Leopold II, 1883

Were our ancestors evil before the colonizer came? The question speaks of my struggle over the years, to reconcile my identity as a Christian and as an African, and also to understand why we were subjected to so much hate and experienced so much suffering. As my life unfolded, I began to pose difficult questions to some of my priests and other religious teachers as I continued on my ongoing journey of transformation. My parents had already passed away, so I had to figure out my own path. Something inside me refuted any notion that the core of my indigenous identity is evil. Deep down, I knew it was wrong to denigrate my people. I intuitively knew they had done a lot of good. Even though I never met a number of them in person, they live on inside me.

Christianity says our ways are evil. I remember watching my grandfather, Denis Gandidzanwa, kneeling on the floor in our dining room. He would speak to the ancestors offering them *mutete* (snuff packaged the Manyika way, in a reed container), letting them know of good news in the family. I saw him do that a few times. I observed quietly. There was nothing sinister about that. So why were our ancestors—and anything having to do with them—condemned as "evil?" I really struggled with the belief that all things African were evil.

As I reflect on my earlier life, I better understand how some people practised Christianity during the day but were African traditional believers at night. It promoted deception and "syncretism" (combining different forms of belief or practice.) I know my parents were not evil. As a child, I never knew about their struggle, likely wrestling with two different belief systems. Now I wonder how they ever managed it? They were generous and beloved in the community. Their love was reciprocated. They were not evil.

Have you ever experienced a spiritual struggle, the sort of a conflict where two belief systems are fighting inside you and you feel like you are being pulled from both ends and therefore not standing on solid ground? If you answered yes, take a minute and write down what you think and how you feel.

Raised predominantly Christian, I realized that I felt an emptiness not knowing enough about African beliefs. The inner spiritual turmoil I experienced stirred within me confusion, guilt, shame. I felt I lacked direction and grounding, especially after I lost my parents in 1992 and 1993. When the core of one's being is attacked, stripped away, it's no wonder people feel lost. I was lost. I knocked on doors I should never have knocked and entered places I should never have entered. My search made me vulnerable to deception and exploitation. Still, my powers of discernment helped me to detect deception. I did encounter evil, but it had nothing to do with traditional African religion. As with any religion, there are good and bad aspects.

My issues with Christianity nagged at me for years, until 2014, when I became an immigrant and settled on Inuit land in the city of Iqaluit in Nunavut, in the Canadian Arctic. ("Inuit" refers to the Arctic indigenous populations of Alaska, Canada, and Greenland. Inuit means "people.)

Inuit share a similar colonial history with my native people. When I heard some of them speaking about "reclaiming" who they are, it made me feel safe to explore. I felt like I had come home; I was in a place where I could talk about the colonizer without people rolling their eyes at me.

In 2017, as I researched being both African and Christian, I stumbled upon a letter on the internet. It helped me answer the nagging question. The letter, by King Leopold II, was written in 1883, addressed to Belgian Christian missionaries on a mission to Congo. An activist from Sierra Leone, Eunice Barber, writing in the *African Globe*, shared that the missionaries were the harbingers of colonization, and that traders and the army would follow. This tied in very well with what happened in Zimbabwe and many other African countries. I share King Leopold's letter below:

Dear Reverends, Fathers and Compatriots,

"The task that you have been given to fulfill is very delicate and requires much tact. You will go certainly to evangelize, but your evangelization must inspire above all Belgium interests. Your principal objective in our mission in the Congo is never to teach the niggers to know God, this they know already. They speak and submit to a Mungu, one Nzambi, one Nzakomba, and what else I don't know.

They know that to kill, to sleep with someone else's wife, to lie and to insult is bad. Have courage to admit it; you are not going to teach them what they know already. Your essential role is to facilitate the task of administrators and industrials, which means you will go to interpret the Gospel in the way it will be the best to protect your interests in that part of the world. For these things, you have to keep watch on disinteresting our savages from the richness that is plenty in their underground. To avoid that, that they get interested in it, and make you murderous competition and dream one day to overthrow you.

Your knowledge of the Gospel will allow you to find texts ordering, and encouraging your followers to love poverty, like "Happier are the poor because they will inherit the heaven" and, "It's very difficult for the rich to enter the kingdom of God." You have to detach from them and make them disrespect everything which gives courage to affront us. I make reference to their Mystic System and their war fetish–warfare protection– which they pretend not to want to abandon, and you must do everything in your power to make it disappear.

Your actions will be directed essentially to the younger ones, for they won't revolt when the recommendation of the priest is contradictory to their parent's teachings. The children have to learn to obey what the missionary recommends, who is the father of their soul. You must singularly insist on their total submission and obedience, avoid developing the spirit in the schools, teach students to read and not to reason.

Convert always the Blacks by using the whip. Keep their women in nine months of submission to work freely for us. Force them to pay you in sign of recognition—goats, chicken or eggs—every time you visit their villages. And make sure that niggers never become rich. Sing every day that it's impossible for the rich to enter heaven. Make them pay tax each week, at Sunday mass. Use the money supposed for the poor, to build flourishing business centres. Institute a confessional system, which allows you to be good detectives denouncing any Black that has a different consciousness contrary to that of the decision-maker. Teach the niggers to forget their heroes and to adore only ours. Never present a chair to a Black that comes to visit you. Don't give him more than one cigarette. Never invite him for dinner even if he gives you a chicken every time you arrive at his house."

Clearly, this letter was supposed to be kept secret, but according to Ms. Barber's account, a Nigerian professor, Dr. Chiedozie Okoro, says it was found in a second-hand Bible. A man named Moukouani Muikwani Bukoko bought it from a Belgian priest who apparently had forgotten the letter was in it. In my interpretation, our "real" God wanted to shame the devil by revealing the hidden truth. God wanted us brainwashed "savages" to be liberated. The truth sets us free. It certainly set my mind free.

While it was heartbreaking to read, I am grateful to have uncovered the truth I had been looking for. I had found the centerpiece of the puzzle. All the internal mind battles I had had wondering why human beings were so cruel to other human beings created in the image of God, ceased. The brutality and the violence I witnessed—and also experienced first-hand in my first decade of life—now made complete sense. It answered a question I had long considered: Why would the Rhodesian government confiscate a vehicle parked in our yard, flatly saying to my father, "a Black person cannot own such a vehicle." It explained why Cecil John Rhodes, the quintessential racist of 'Rhodesia', could use God to justify colonizing Africa. As he said, "If there be a God, I think that what He would, like me, paint as much of the map of Africa British Red as possible".

It had nothing to do with our God, Musikavanhu or Mwari in Shona, Mungu, Nzambi or Nzakomba, as Leopold had researched. What Rhodes said helped me to reconcile what is happening with white supremacists in the US today. They profess to believe in God but are propagators of hate. Since our ideas of God are not the same, I fail to comprehend those "men of God".

There was a time when I hated to hear the expression, "Religion is the opium of the masses;" after reading King Leopold's letter it totally made sense. We were opiated; many of us still are. Imagine the betrayal I felt knowing that the very religion I was born into was actually used for mind control and outright evil. It stripped us of our first line of defence, our culture. Anger roiled inside; confusion gripped me. I wanted to know why at church we were never told about such things and why apologies for this heinous robbery of our identity had never been proffered. When those thoughts assailed me, I would talk with my sister Tina, and she would say, "Let's not go there." Her suggestion? It was best for us to not rock the boat. Meanwhile, I began to ask, "So who are we and why do we still go to church?" It messed up our heads. I bet my bottom dollar we were not alone!

There is no doubt that many Africans whose ancestors converted to Christianity are not only rethinking their allegiance to that religion but are also both exploring and reclaiming their connection to African traditional religions. In her article, Eunice Barber was blunt in her assessment of how true stories impacted Africans. She wrote: "Thanks to a century or more of this Leopold-mandated missionary mind control, African Christians are not an activist, self-helping, economically engaged, politically resolute—let alone militant—bunch. Hence, their putting up with all manner of mistreatment and exploitation by their *mis*rulers, white and Black."

It is on record: Africans *can* rise up and fight. The sad reality though, is that there is evidence that many post-independence African leaders, like their colonial masters, now use the same methods to oppress their own people. Africa today, though rich in some ways, is still engulfed by poverty, even as most of its leaders live opulent lifestyles. The mind control was not only handy for the colonizer. It continues under today's rulers; they have been coopted into valuing money over human life.

Also, like their colonial rulers, they have mastered the art of employing police brutality, strategically using intelligence operatives to terrorize their own people. They whip and abduct fellow Africans for speaking out against injustice. They manipulate education and religion to keep people docile. "Pray, and stay away from politics," they cynically counsel. The majority of our leaders prefer fear to love. That is the tragedy of the human race. It must be countered: the spirit of Ubuntu, "I am because you are," must prevail!

I now understand why we Africans are preyed upon by deceptive Christians; among them pastors, prophets, and apostles, who unashamedly steal from the poor. We were opiated. We are still opiated. We need to wake up! Those who are awake and try to awaken their duped brothers and sisters meet with their wrath as they profess, "Touch not the anointed." You know, the brothers and sisters have done crazy things like drinking "anointed" bleach, eating "anointed" grass, applying "anointed" oil and having their genitalia touched.

Such brainwashed devotees tithe exorbitant amounts to their church and leave their families hungry. They condone sexual abuse and sweep allegations under the carpet. Their churches operate like cults. Some *are*, in fact, cults, which have for centuries practiced mind control over their congregants. Undoing mind control is not a walk in the park. Among other things, it requires speaking the truth, and many are not ready for God's real truth.

Too many of us operate at the "magical" level of consciousness, relinquishing our undesired reality to some supernatural power and, as a consequence, believe we are powerless to change our reality. We expect miracles—that God will change our reality without our active participation in changing our undesired reality socially, politically and economically. We need to wake up! There is no transformation without radical action, and radical means going to the root.

In Nunavut, the wounds that the church inflicted on Inuit are still fresh. The more than 1000 Indigenous children of Canada, whose voices refused to be silenced, speak from the graves discovered in 2021. They are testimony to the paradoxical role religion has played in destroying the gift of life and opiating people.

I have witnessed Inuit grapple with social challenges, just as have my sisters and brothers in Zimbabwe. Just as they did back home, the colonizers intentionally destroyed the native peoples' source of livelihood, forcing them to live in settlements and adopt a "civilized" (read conventional, western way) of living. That has made me realize how our education system glossed over both the impact of colonization *and* how we see the world. The remnants of colonialism are still entrenched in societies; it explains why systemic injustice still prevails. Racism is alive in its various strains around the world.

God was already in Africa

The culture of silence is real. The loss of identity has caused intergenerational trauma. People experience intergenerational emotional systems of anxiety, depression, worry, frustration, sadness, anger and fear—all a direct result of colonization. Same impact, different geography. And, as opiated people, many of us still think the colonizer did us a favour by establishing schools, and "allowing" us to function in their wage economy. The questions we don't want to answer back home include, "What type of education have we been provided?" Whose curriculum were they teaching us, and in whose language? And for whose benefit?

King Leopold's letter clearly instructed, "teach students to read and not to reason." Have you ever blindly believed what you were taught? We have a tendency to underestimate the opiating impact of education. I have learnt that without asking critical questions, we fall prey to the oppressor's schemes and remain oppressed. For example, we must begin to question the efficacy of a 'standard' education. We were brainwashed to think it's the best that could happen to us. I wonder what might have happened if the colonizer had not disrupted the way people lived, imposing their so-called superior lifestyle? We would have evolved, but we cannot tell how. Now we are forced to be grateful to those that "brought us up by hand," as Dickens says in *Great Expectations*. At least I speak and write very good English, so I must be grateful.

With my question answered, I have freed myself from my identity dilemma. I am carving out my own spirituality; it acknowledges my African culture and roots and permits me to relate to my ancestors my way, unapologetically singing my traditional songs as well as composing Christian songs, all on the same mbira. I have learnt that if our faiths rely on fear, comparison, and separation—and instil in us a sense of superiority—our worship is using saboteur energy. Our religion is no longer in its pure essence. We can turn this around by operating from a non-judgmental, non-fear-mongering perspective guided by unconditional love. My new spirituality allows me to commune with others of different faiths without judgment and endorses my guiding principle of love.

God was already in Africa. Leopold knew that our people knew God but in our own languages, in our own way. When I played the African drum at our small church, congregants from all over the world told me how it spoke to them. The drums heal.

Sometimes, I wear traditional headwear associated with my ancestors. When I do, I no longer feel guilty or ashamed. No one can tell me that my ancestors are evil. They called God, Musikavanhu, the creator of people, or Muari or Mwari, the "one in whom I am."

I do not believe in the blue-eyed, white poster boy of western religion who, with the help of hegemonic forces, has masqueraded as Jesus Christ. *That* deity advances white superiority and aids in perpetuating racial inequality. Those forces refuse to acknowledge that Jesus was bronze in complexion.

We have been manipulated, told to believe everything preached is the "gospel truth". We fail to recognize that the word of God is abused to advance the agenda of human beings. We tend to trust those who purport to help us, and we end up being taken advantage of because we never question why some people *want* to help us, whether as wealthy individuals, families, communities; even countries.

If continents and countries were male, we would have to acknowledge that Africa was castrated. If female, we would say the continent has been raped multiple times. First, by the colonizer, a stranger; second, by her own family. Africa must be healed; she must not remain opiated. The remnants of racial discrimination that Africa fought against for so long, has reared its ugly head. The economic system within which we all operate was designed to benefit a few rich people. It has not transformed in the aftermath of Africa being partitioned. The money is still in the hands of wealthy former colonizers and superpowers; they still wield power, still make the decisions, even though Africa has all the mineral wealth. It's being traded for a song, by design.

Mallence Bart Williams articulates my perspective—what is in my heart—clearly and powerfully, in her powerful 2015 Ted Talk, "Change Your Channel." There she exposed the paradox of wealthy nations that print paper money based on mineral wealth from African soil while simultaneously—and shamelessly—labeling Africa as poor.

Here is the new, evangelized message for Africans and descendants of Africa. *Wake up Africa! Speak up Africa! Wise up Africa! Rise up Africa!* Racial superiority is what enabled King Leopold and his followers to mistreat their fellow human beings without remorse. They pounced strategically, with laser-focused intention and precision. Race as a divisive device is still alive, overtly and covertly, and will remain a handy tool for those seeking power and glory at all cost.

I do not know what your journey has been like, but this is my story as one of the racially oppressed. Perhaps you are like me, someone whose life was undermined; or, maybe, you are on the other side, a beneficiary of racial inequality. Moving forward, you have a choice to make. As you read this book, I invite you to be curious, to explore and reflect on your reality. I share my "gospel" of racial equality from an Afrocentric perspective, and my experience of racism in both the southern and northern hemisphere. Come with me on my journey to liberate myself.

CHAPTER THREE

"Black" is Not a Skin Colour

February 2018. There were about 70 of us in the Anglican Parish Hall in the city of Iqaluit, thousands of miles from my native Zimbabwe. The smell of African cuisine from multiple countries filled the air. My stomach growled and my mouth watered anticipating digging into some delicious food from back home. Rhumba music from Meiway, the acclaimed singer from Côte d'Ivoire, was booming from the sound system.

I had landed in Iqaluit, in the Territory of Nunavut, on Christmas Eve, 2014. I had been someone who had vowed to never leave Zimbabwe, but political, social, and emotional circumstances intervened. To be blunt, I was forced to run for my life—a life I nearly had terminated earlier that year. When my sisters living in North America said they wanted to help extricate me from the jaws of death, I couldn't refuse.

As someone who had come back from the brink of suicide, *I* had been a danger to my life, but not the only danger. I had received death threats; indeed, one was made in front of my family.

I received the lethal threat after I had sent a government minister's wife a Mother's Day message. "If, as mothers, we all told our sons not to participate in election violence," I wrote, "no mother would be mourning the death of her child. Happy Mothers Day." She viciously responded, promising to send Central Intelligence Officers after me and, true to her word, they came. It was not my first or last encounter with the system.

In another incident, a bloodshot-eyed officer from the criminal investigations department, sat in my car interrogating me, accusing me of being a politician, as if that was a crime. He was supposed to be helping us recover stolen property. When I told him, "If you have been sent to kill me, you will be doing me a favour. You will be fast-tracking me to heaven. We will meet six feet under, because what I am doing is my purpose; I work for justice and peace". He let me go. As was the case with many, many others, because I worked as a human rights educator and activist, we were viewed as teaching subversive content.

It was beginning to take its toll on my body, mind and soul. I began to shift from being a die-hard Zimbabwean to a potential willing emigrant.

It was a relief to leave that kind of stress and move to a peaceful, if very cold, new home. As frigid as it is, there is more warmth in Iqaluit—a place where, with the wind chill factored in, the temperature can drop to minus 59 degrees Celsius—than in Zimbabwe, where the sun shines nearly every day. Sadly, that sun could give me neither peace of mind nor safety of body.

Back to the celebration. More than a few waists were wiggling and multiple pairs of feet were stepping out. Most of us were dressed in colourful outfits typical of our African heritage. When

Africans meet in celebration of culture, it's always colourful and celebratory and—heh heh—*really* loud.

Hugs and kisses were in abundance and a warm feeling of togetherness engulfed the room. There were nearly as many languages spoken as there were people, but who cared? It was Black History Month and we were celebrating both our diverse cultures *and* our common values, our humanity: *I am because you are.* It was a when-I-see-you, I-see-me kind of celebration. We are one. The spirit of Africa was strong that night; it *is* strong.

I was busy chatting with Nadine, a member of our church, and a French-speaking African sister, when her eight-year-old son, Azriel, came up to me stretching his left hand and touching his caramel skin, running his finger up and down. Looking at me, he said, "Aunty, why should I agree to be called black when my skin is brown? At school, my friends keep forcing me to say that I am black." I paused and wondered what I would say to him.

Has a child ever asked you questions about race? How have you answered? At that moment, my brain was working double time. What do I tell this child? What is the best answer that is going to wipe clean the confusion and sadness on his face? Should *I* even answer it with his mother standing right next to me? Wouldn't it be better to tell him to ask his mother? But he chose to address you, I reminded myself. The rebel aunty in me said, "You are brown, son. You should tell them that you do not like being called 'black' because clearly, if it is about skin colour, you are not black!" His eyes brightened.

"Thank you Aunty, because I do not like it." He made a little happy dance and ran off to resume playing with the other children. As an aunty, I felt happy that I had told a truth that set that child free, at least in that moment. I knew it was not going to be an easy road for him, especially since other children would no doubt seek to shroud him in undesired blackness; try to force him to accept a false identity. What I know is he was sure about what his eyes saw and how he wanted to be addressed. He just needed confirmation, affirmation.

I was sad for him. It reminded me how a few months earlier some boys his age, six or seven, had shouted "nigger!" and followed me as I walked along Frobisher Bay beach in the city of Iqaluit near the Nunatta Sunakkutaangit Museum. I remember seeing adults standing by their balconies looking on. I remained quiet and walked away, feeling sad. I wondered if such boys went to the same school as Azriel. He is a strong-minded, resolute boy. My prayer is he keeps believing in himself and defining his own identity. That is the life of our African children.

I wonder how many of these little ones might be asking themselves questions about why they are being discriminated against and how confused they must be? Faced with difficult questions, we have a tendency to teach our children the race lies that we were taught. We continue to repeat the programming we went through, including the race binary and because of that, we might be unintentionally passing on hate.

Yes, people who look like me are taught that we are Black. We have a month dedicated to "Black" history. It is written in books that we are Black, but for eight-year-old Azriel, "Black" does not describe him. He does not like how it feels when others force him to "admit" he is Black. It is not true. It does not matter that it is in the legislation, on immigration forms, in books, speeches, and films, and in the names of organizations that fight for our rights. The identifier is simply not true. Black is not the colour of my skin or Azriel's.

We all know that there is neither black nor white skin, but generation after generation has tainted our children's innocence by passing on both lies and hate. People who look like me have owned "blackness" fiercely, perhaps because it was imposed, not that we had a choice to refuse the label. Some say, "We have owned it and given it power." For me, Black is a political statement not a skin colour.

As we continue to celebrate "Black" History Month, among the questions I have are: "Why were we celebrating one month of history about us when we live "Black history" every day? Why not every month? Why is it so hard to find an accurate history of people who look like us in school curricula? Why should we be grateful to be acknowledged in the month of February?"

For my first three years in Canada, Black History celebrations had been fun, but I had started to question the whole idea of suddenly having to get used to being referred to as "Black", something which was no longer happening back home in Zimbabwe. In passively accepting the label, we could say we did not know better, but maybe now we can't justify that response, especially knowing that children are pushing back. What would you choose, lies or truth? I refuse to perpetuate the lie. Isn't it time to challenge the status quo?

While we ought to be grateful to Carter G. Woodson for founding Negro History Week in 1926—which evolved into black history month, and Black Heritage Month in 1976—it is high time to demand more than just a month acknowledging the history of our ancestors!

In a positive development on the other side of Canada, Nova Scotia has changed its commemoration from Black History Month to African Heritage Month. It embraces all African peoples in

Canada and throughout North America, without mentioning skin colour.

Nadine and I laughed off the exchange and continued our idle talk, but not about race. Still, my mind was sparking again. Honestly, I thought, was this child prophetic? Of all the people he could have chosen to ask, why did he ask me? He had no clue what was coming later that night. I had my mbira with me, and I was wearing my black jumpsuit and black and white zebra print scarf. Black and white means a lot to me as the Zebra is my totem animal. When I am dressed like that, I am proud of that aspect of my identity. The bold contrast between the black and white stripes is beautiful; when the cloth kisses my chocolate skin it reminds me of my true colour and confirms my conviction. I am not Black.

Ify Chiwetelu, a Canadian Broadcast Company anchor in Manitoba, reached out to me saying she was looking for stories about "Black creatives." I was excited to be known that far away! I agreed to be interviewed and made a commitment to myself not to hold back from telling her my opinions of Black History month and my feelings toward being referred to as "Black." I shared that there was a vibrant community of people who look like me and she wanted to know if she could film me among them.

My people said it was fine and that is how I came to perform that night. After I took to the stage, the sound of my mbira filled the room. "*Mhoroi. Makadini, Salibonani, Linjani, Ndimatsheloni, Mahwa tshini. Muriwadi here? Bonjour, Hello, Qanuipi?*" It is a song of welcome, a greeting song. I include as many languages as I can and have added Chinese, Japanese, Spanish, Italian, Hebrew, Tswana, Nyanja and Kiswahili.

As I braced to play my controversial protest song, "Charcoal and Snow", I felt both excitement and fear; excitement to be voicing my feelings, and fear of being rejected by my fellow Africans. I shifted my position and sat upright. I placed my hands on the mbira blades, unsure if I would get the simple pattern right. I summoned my signature smile and set my fearless face. I could feel the song flowing through my fingers and the confidence to sing it out arrived just in time. I certainly did not want to embarrass myself in front of the CBC crew recording me, let alone my sister and brother Africans!

> **Charcoal and Snow**
> *Charcoal and snow*
> *Charcoal and snow*
> *Charcoal and snow ooo.*
>
> *From the bottom rung of the race ladder*
> *there is an African woman who owes herself resilience.*
> *From the bottom rung of the race ladder*
> *there is an African man who owes himself resilience.*
> *Charcoal and snow*
> *Charcoal and snow*
> *Charcoal and snowww ooo.*
>
> *Have you ever seen a person as white as snow?*
> *or as black as charcoal?*
> *Charcoal and Snow*
> *Charcoal and snow,*
> *Charcoal and snow ooo*
>
> *In primary school when the teacher was writing, the chalk was white and the blackboard was black.*

I am talking about
Charcoal and snow
Charcoal and snow
Charcoal and snow ooo.

When I was asked to draw myself in primary school, I picked dark brown for the colour of my skin, not black

I am talking about charcoal and snow,
Charcoal and snow, charcoal and snow ooo.

I am talking about charcoal and snow.
I am talking about charcoal and snow
I am not black, and you are not white!
I am not black, and you are not white.

I knew my words were going to disrupt people and, true to my suspicions, I had some reactions from my sisters and brothers. Still, some knew the depth of my feelings— what I meant by refusing the label "Black." I might disrupt you, too, if you look like me and you love your Black label. Please remember I promised not to impose any labels on you.

The lingering question on my mind is, "At what cost to humanity are we keeping our "blackness" and our "whiteness?" Remember the expression, "Tell a lie enough times and it begins to sound true." Lies have a price tag. Those labels are not mere words; they carry energy and, for some, privilege. For others, nothing but disadvantage.

Language matters. What would happen if race lies were banned? Are we afraid of losing our identity? Does the race binary serve certain people so well that they cannot imagine a life without it? The big question: Who benefits from imposing, accepting and agreeing to racial identity?

Many see the safest path is going along with the so-called majority position because we fear being ostracized. We want to identify with a group, with people who look like us, (or, who were indoctrinated the same as us). When our need for identity is so strong that we are prepared to ignore the voices of children and those in the minority, what does that mean?

For me, the lies that our ancestors were coerced into believing will not imprison me in a fake identity that they may have believed they were powerless to refute. But I am not. I am tired of swallowing an identity that has been shoved down my throat; an identity that does not describe who I am. I am tired of hearing those old tropes, "We have always been called Black" and "We have always done it that way."

I trust what I feel and "Black" has no place when I describe who I am! At the same time, I am not going to force my ideas on anyone, especially those who feel attached and have crafted their lives around blackness. Nevertheless, the objective truth must be told. I am willing to stand in my own truth, which I call God's truth. I know the stakes are high.

I am a future ancestor who does not fit into the boxes of charcoal and snow, black and white. When an African man and a Caucasian woman have a baby, that child also does not fit into a black or white box. They should not have to, but the world—at least the one we are living in now—forces them to.

Back to the gathering. We had in our midst that night a Caucasian French woman married to one of our African brothers. When people kept saying, "This [gathering] is for us Black people", I looked out for her, afraid she might feel unwelcome. I also looked at her son, neither white nor Black, innocently playing with the other children. Watching him reminded me that the fight must go on. These colours deprive us of human connection and love. I vowed that I would do my part. Our grandchildren should never feel that they are not "Black enough", "Asian enough" or "white enough." They should never feel they must tick the "right" boxes where they will never quite fit. Humanity is richer than that; you are richer than that—and so am I.

I refuse to remain in victim mode, angry, hijacked, and potentially dangerous, to myself and others, especially my loved ones. I release toxic emotions and pain and breathe in possibility. When my thoughts go into deep, troubling waters, playing mbira is the medicine that cures me from negativity.

After the heaviness of singing about race, I ended my performance with a happier song, "Ndoenda KuDiaspora", both funny and melodic. I was glad to care for people's feelings, closing with a positive, feel-good song.

The truth is liberating. I sing it. I write it. I speak it. It is the only key to real transformation. Racial equality can only be possible when we open up to the truth and liberate ourselves from the boxes in which the system tries to neatly package us.

Are you willing to be truthful? Are you willing to be an authentic equal? Are you willing to delve deeper than your assigned skin colour, to look in the mirror and show your true colour to the world? *All* your true colours? Are you willing to be part of the change we need to humanize the world? The change I am talking about can only come about by speaking your truth, your authentic words, and committing to loving yourself and others unconditionally. I am willing. Are you?

Try this exercise: Go to the mirror and look at yourself and say out loud the real colour of your skin. Reflect on your assigned skin colour and what it means to you. What are you becoming aware of? What do you think? How do you feel? Let the truth sink in. For me the lesson is, do not automatically accept and agree with race lies. Will you join me in saying, "No" to the imposition of labels? I hope so.

In 2016, I worked part time as a cashier at a grocery store. I had an Indian boss who was very understanding and great to work with. One day he said to me, "You *Black* people…" as we were talking about our countries and cultures. I stopped him right there and went to his side. "Show me your hand, sir." He did. I put my hand next to his. "What colour is your hand?" I asked. "Brown," he replied. "What colour is mine? Again he replied, "Brown." Our shades were nearly the same. He was shocked. "Do not call me "black" or use the phrase 'you Black people' ever again! Call me African. If you want to know about my culture, country or continent, just ask."

Taha, a Pakistani-Canadian immigrant brother, who "gets" me, and who understands what I mean by "I am not black", sent me a picture captioned, "Black is not a skin colour." Below it was this poem:

> **Black**
>
> Black is not the colour of a skin
> Black cannot ride in posh cars
> Or look with contempt on the poor
> The hand is black that wields a machete
> Cutting sugar so that others may grow rich
> Black sleeps rough
> In corrugated iron shanty-towns
> Black tilling the soil, is drained

By the vampire landlord
But raises a voice of revolt
Black grips the guns and the knives
To bring down the well off and the mighty
Black is the colour of a heart.

(*From the first issue of* Kala Mazdoor, *a magazine addressing racism, the right to self-defence, and the struggle against immigration control.*)

He also sent me a screen shot from a brown history page, *The Politics of Britain's Asian Youth Movements*, by Anandi Ramamurhy.

I was fascinated by the fact that "if you were to look at historical videos and photos of South Asian movements against racism during the 1970s and '80s in Britain, you would notice many of them identified as "Black." It can be seen in the poems, signs, banners, posters and fliers. It's because through their experiences with oppression (police brutality, racist landlords, white supremacist groups, hate-mongering politicians and unfair immigration controls, South Asians felt united with Africans and African Caribbeans. At the time Black was not seen as a skin colour but a political colour."

I pray—and work—for the return of such solidarity and, even better than that, the unity of all humans. History should be history without a colour. Black history, brown history, white history. Why assign colour to it?

CHAPTER FOUR

Letter to Prime Minister Justin Trudeau

> *"Race and status are defined by the dominant group in society politically, economically, socio-culturally, and historically and is propped by collective acceptance, agreement, and imposition."*
> —Prof. Dana Osborne, Department of Languages, Literatures and Cultures, Ryseron University, Toronto

By 2017, it was becoming a struggle for me to stomach the insults that were hurled at me because of how I look. Nunavut, my happy place, had a few people who managed to grieve me to the point of impacting my mental health. It happened enough times for me to know it was time to radically act, to change my reality.

I was tired of being called "nigger" and "black thing." I was tired of being told, "Go back to Africa." I was tired of being told

I did not know what I was doing at work, only for my accusers to realize I was right after all and then apologize— before the cycle started all over. I was tired of being terrorized, publicly humiliated while my abusers were praised in front of me for work *I* had done.

I was tired of being told to go to Nova Scotia, the province where "black" people in Canada live in greater numbers, to access grants and loans to help me, an immigrant mother, finance my son's dream of becoming a pilot. Since the system didn't have real help for my people; that was the best advice they could offer me.

I wanted the person who held the highest office in the country to know that while Canada prides itself for recognizing diversity, as an African, I did not feel protected from community and systemic racism. I wanted race issues to be addressed holistically, and that meant paying attention to anti-Black racism, too. I say black for lack of a better term.

I asked myself, "What bold action could I take to confront this injustice?" The answer came in a flash: contact the prime minister, Justin Trudeau! He had the power. I had met him and had taken a selfie with him in the city of Iqaluit when he was running for office. He was a charming, accessible personality, attentive and sharp. I trusted he would hear me and do something about such an important topic. After all, he had achieved 50/50 gender parity when he appointed his cabinet in

2015. His step towards gender equality was recognized around the world.

I knew, too, that his office was responsive. Previously, they had communicated with me in a timely manner when I had requested my children be allowed to join me in Canada. Although the response was not what I had wanted, his office had heard me, even offering advice on an alternative way to get my children admitted into the country. If I poured my heavy heart out to Prime Minister Trudeau, I told myself, I felt confident I would be heard. Here is the letter I sent him on 20 February 2018.

Your Excellency, Prime Minister Trudeau,

I hope this mail finds you well. Please accept my letter in this, Black History month. It is my hope that you will personally read it and will hear my message and do everything in your power to change the race narrative in Canada and hopefully the rest of the world.

I have attached photos so that you put faces to the message I have shared with you. I appreciate Inuit for being on their land, and Canada for giving me refuge and a source of livelihood and opportunities for my children. I hope my passion and advocacy will be regarded as a positive and constructive thing for Canada.

I write to you with respect as the leader of the country that gave me a home when I needed peace in my life. For that I am eternally grateful.

Today, I request you, as the leader of Canada, lead the world in the deconstruction of race. It is a scary subject often only scratched on the surface; never addressed from the root. I do think it is time for a world leader to change the race narrative for good. You, your Excellency, are capable of doing it.

Below are my reasons that explain why I know you are capable of achieving this critically important goal.

1. Race is just a construct, a lie, not a fact, so if the truth be told, race can be deconstructed. The colours white and Black as racial groups are not consistent with the range of human diversity and the multiple skin colours and tones we have in the world; yet to date the primary race indicator is skin color.

2. I recognize that that racism is entrenched not only in the minds of people, but it is also propagated and entrenched in all institutions responsible for socialization, beginning in families, then schools, churches, cultural groups, sporting and other social groups, and the media. Race pervades legal systems, prison systems, and educational systems, housing systems, employment systems, immigration systems and many more societal structures; hence the entire system ought to be transformed. All histories, including the true history of Black and Aboriginal people, can be given weight and be taught as part of the education system's curriculum from kindergarten through university. The judiciary, the legislature and the executive play a pivotal role in this kind of transformation and that is where you, as our leader, comes in.

3. You have started to make reforms for Aboriginal people and that gives me hope and shows your responsiveness to racism. However, as a so-called Black person, it is my wish that race be dealt with in a holistic manner, covering all other people of diverse identities impacted by its pervasive and divisive nature. Here in Canada, I have suffered racial violence and discrimination by some Inuit and French males.

   Also a well-known white, female bully victimized not only me but many others in my workplace. Mine just took a more intense twist. My sister Tina was called, 'You black thing'—when she was pregnant—by another woman because she had said she did not have money to buy the wares she was selling. We had to swallow the insults hurled at all of us. (This incident happened in a restaurant here in Iqaluit where we had gone to celebrate a milestone—Tina surviving a very complicated pregnancy.) In my view, all social strata created by the construct of race must be addressed. Everyone must know that each person is a human being and if they expect racial justice then they must be just themselves.

4. The application of "race" as a concept has been, since its inception, inextricably linked to power," as Osborne observed. You are the power holder and therefore you can choose to use that power to influence how the race narrative will be in future in Canada and, hopefully, the rest of the world.

5. According to Osborne, "race and status are defined by the dominant group in society politically, economically,

socio-culturally, and *historically* is propped up by collective acceptance, agreement, and imposition." Many "black and white" people are oblivious to their tacit agreement to and acceptance of race. Fanon says while white people claim that they are anti-racist, they partake in a racialized system and do not see the privileges they have simply due to their skin colour.

6. Today, if you, as a leader, refuse to perpetuate the colours that symbolize superiority and inferiority in the human race and consequently accords social status, people will listen to you and change can happen sooner than we might imagine. I believe that race justice, just like gender justice, calls for changing the labels black and white-the race binary.

Let me share a few more Nunavut race stories and what I am doing. I share an office—as well as my stories of pain on a daily basis—with an Inuk. We share many things in common and realize we are more similar than different. Our levels of consciousness are more or less the same, believing in holistic approaches to our work. After he read the attachment I am sending to you, "I Am Not Black", he paused for a long time and asked me, "So what is race?"

He told me about a murdered Indigenous woman who was mistaken for a white woman, as he normally is. The response and support the parents of the woman got from the RCMP while the deceased was assumed to be white was great. As soon as it became known that she was Inuit, the support diminished.

We shared more experiences of systemic racism and injustices. I have still not figured out what color Inuit are because in Africa, they would be regarded as "white." They call themselves "Inuit" meaning people, and in my culture we call ourselves "Vanhu" or "Abantu", also meaning people. To both of us, racial classification is a colonial concept that diminishes our social standing and excludes us from participating in the social, economic and political spheres as equals.

At a gathering of African and Caribbean people on 10 February 2018, I said that in the next 100 years I would not want my grandchildren to be talking about "black and white" but rather about the human race. We have long had interracial couples. We do not want to keep having awkward relationships and children who don't have a box to tick because they are neither Black nor white.

Race intersects with gender and class; we all experience it differently. It is complex; still, we all have a role to play. In 2017, I connected with people of diverse identities here in Iqaluit to show people that we can live in harmony despite our differences. We performed during "Toonik time" (the Inuit celebration of the coming of the sun) and we called our act CanaDiversity. I have been talking to Taha Tabish who was also part of CanaDiversity about beginning the race work that is long overdue here and, of course, everywhere in the world. In Iqaluit we are already meeting. We need your support.

We know that if we all use the gifts we have to tackle the issue, we shall overcome. In my quest to decolonize knowledge, I am currently conducting research on Africans in Nunavut to ensure that the history we are making here will be told by us. As Fanon did, I do believe that race can be tackled and perhaps our grandchildren may live in a non-racialized world.

I have faith in your government, and I hope that you can

visualize the truth we need to tell about our skin colours and to sit in the discomfort that that truth brings us, hoping that after we are done, real transformation will be the yield.

Sincerely,
Francisca Mandeya

> I must confess that in retrospect, I have felt my judge and anger saboteur in some parts of the letter. I had not yet been trained as a solution-focused and positive intelligence coach; otherwise I would have expressed myself in a more positive or sage way. I have since forgiven myself.

I am not sure Prime Minister Trudeau ever saw my letter, let alone read it. What I am sure of is I did not get the response I had wished for. I was hurting and I wanted assurance that I mattered, and that people who look like me mattered, too.

When in 2018 the issue of the prime minister having once worn blackface surfaced during his campaign for a second term, all I could think of was I sure wished he had read my letter and taken my message seriously. He might have preempted the issue that obviously worked against him. The media reported, "There are least three photos and one video of Trudeau wearing racist makeup." In his response to the report, he confessed: "I take responsibility for my decision to do that. I shouldn't have done it," he said. "I should have known better. It was something that I didn't think was racist at the time, but now I recognize it was something racist to do and I am deeply sorry."

After reading the apology, I accepted it. I had compassion for him because of my personal experience with him. Many

Canadians said that wearing a black or brown face was just part of a costume. I agreed with them. It did not hurt me to hear what he did. The deed was racist but I hesitated to label him.

I came to the realization that sometimes our innocence and ignorance can lead us to do or say things that are hurtful or offensive to others. That is why it is important to ensure that education includes the true history of people so that we can come from our highest selves as empowered people who treat each other equally and justly.

I have also learnt that many of us have a tendency to judge ourselves, others, and life itself, negatively. Our inner critics, our "nasty judges", are capable of destroying us, and others. There might be no photo or video evidence of our racist thoughts, words and deeds, but we all have them. Therefore, it is with caution that I criticize and label others. I am aware of my dark side and my nasty judge. I commit daily to being empathetic and increasing my light. I am also aware of the inner warrior who steps up and in to fight for what is right and just.

What I like about leaders who apologize is that their vulnerability is powerful. They inspire the people they lead to do what is right. The part about not knowing better opens possibilities for the prime minister—or any leader, for that matter—to convert his or her experience into a gift, an opportunity for systemic transformation.

Political leaders wield the power to transform undesired realities. I have seen PM Trudeau move the gender equality agenda forward with passion and conviction. At Women Deliver, the biggest gender equality conference in the world, I heard him say, "Diversity is a fact; inclusion is a choice." The choice I pray he makes regarding Black or "brown" people is to listen deeply and thereafter work with those populations to make systemic reforms that will go a long way to walk towards racial equality.

I call on global leaders to prioritize: give the same prominence to racial equality as you do for gender equality. As I make my intentions to work for racial justice and equality clear, I invite everyone to be anti-racist. It takes love for us to be able to acknowledge our part, to own it, and to transform the ugly reality of racial injustice. Everyone has a role to play.

CHAPTER FIVE

Is There Racism in the Workplace?

Work must be fun because we spend so much time there.

The light in my eyes was extinguished; darkness took over as a swirling tornado of negativity pummeled me. The fierce fighter in me was seething with anger, debating whether to stage a full-blown drama, or find a better way to deal with white arrogance and ignorance.

Six foot, two-inch "Mr. Brown", the name I'm assigning to a manager in a division that worked closely with mine, towered above me. He might as well have been speaking into a megaphone as he proclaimed my ignorance for all to hear throughout our open workspace. "Franchesca! You do not know what you are doing. This is wrong!"

One person in the "audience" was a human resources officer whose office was across from mine. I was dumbfounded. I couldn't believe someone would make such a rude, uncalled for accusation, especially when, in fact, I *did* know what I was doing. The HR officer shot me a look that conveyed she understood what was happening. She walked away with a knowing nod. Still, I thought, what good is an ally, if she isn't willing to speak up in the face of injustice?

Have you ever found yourself asking the question, "What is wrong with me?" You know there is nothing wrong, but you ask anyway. Self-doubt is so detrimental to our mental health that it can send one down a dangerous trail. I was supposed to be this intelligent woman who delivers at work instead I felt dumb, worthless. I made sure to check my work several times before I confirmed there was nothing wrong. The only person who was wrong was Mr. Brown. Even with that knowledge, I couldn't even get up for tea break for fear of being seen by coworkers who had heard me being belittled and shamed.

I decided to respond to Mr. Brown in an email. I sent him proof of what I had done and showed him where he was wrong. He did not respond in writing, but later came to my workspace and said, "I guess you were right. Apologies." I accepted the apology, but that was not the end. He repeated it in the presence of my supervisor who attempted to diffuse the tension, encouraging us with the words, "Let's just serve." I couldn't leave it there. I refused to be silenced, protesting, "I know what I am doing and will not accept Mr. Brown talking to me this way." The two men looked at each other and there was silence. I proceeded to "serve" but I was incensed. I have found that words tend to land on people's hearts in ways that can be life-giving or life-taking. The negativity of Mr. Brown's attacks was beginning to squeeze the confidence—and life—out of me.

I contacted HR. A staff member advised me that if I wanted to press charges, Mr. Brown would be found wanting. He was instructed to apologize but I learnt that he'd said he could not get himself to apologize to me, instead apologizing to my African supervisor. Did he think that would suffice? Wow! Was I dealing with racism as well as sexism? The twin "isms" triggered double rage. I took ten days off to cool down and, in that period, wisdom whispered to me, "It is not you. It is him who needs help." I made a promise to myself, "Keep your head high. Look him in the face and greet him when you cross paths. Do not look down as if you are guilty of anything. Take back your power. Do not allow him to change who you are."

I had another tense encounter with a different male in a different workplace. When I approached my supervisor to express my grievance, her comment was, "Oh, did he do that? He must have been stressed." That was it, even though he had bullied me in front of colleagues *and* had commanded me to change a presentation I had prepared. He mentioned the name of a senior member of the organization's hierarchy who looked like him and said, "She will not understand what you have presented, so you need to change it." His voice growing louder, he barked, "*Change it now!*" His face was red, his voice threatening. Tension mounted, but I refused to back down. I told him he was free to change the presentation and sign it himself. I saw one of my colleague's eyes well up with tears. She felt the pain for me. I blinked back my own tears. I steeled myself. I was not going to cry in public.

Life can be a nightmare if your work environment is not healthy and safe. This job had been the safest, yet for two weeks I felt a constant pain in my chest. Once again, I had been hijacked by a deep sadness washing over me. My self-esteem, my self-confidence, my morale all plummeted. I did not understand my loss of drive. I loved my work, but I didn't like going *to* work anymore. My experiences left me asking, "How can a human being treat a person this way and fail to understand the damage they are causing?" When I shared my experiences with a knowledgeable consultant I knew, her answer rang true: "Our white privilege." She touched me deeply with her readiness to confront racism without being defensive.

She was the opposite of a woman I'll call "Ms. Troller." She was a privileged white woman whose name I have changed to protect her. I worked with her when I was on a three-month renewable contract. As a single, immigrant, African mother. I needed the job. My children's futures depended on me giving them a good education. I had to make sure I renewed my contract and I put my heart into my work. It was common knowledge that Ms. Troller had been placed in her powerful supervisory position because of her connections, not her credentials, and certainly not her interpersonal skills. She saw herself as the center of the world. No one was supposed to outshine her. She was untouchable. She wielded power and she played on the power differential.

One day, Ms. Troller embarrassed me in the presence of her subordinate, and they both regularly ridiculed me over minor things. She blamed me for a communication breakdown even though it was someone else's mistake. No matter what work I did—and that others may have congratulated me for doing well—she only saw mistakes. She was always pushing my buttons.

She sometimes would intentionally pass through my workspace with another senior manager, "whispering" loud enough for me to hear, criticizing documents I had written, or bad-mouthing other people. To deal with the impact of this drama, I would have a good laugh, likening them to nasty high school pom-pom girls. I felt a little bit safe as my ally, an imposing white, was stationed across the aisle. Another ally, an Inuk lady, refused to silently stand by when she heard the two managers gossiping about "the lazy African." She told them about all the work I had done. I am grateful for her standing up for me, something too many people fear to do in the face of injustice. Nevertheless, the two women did not stop their microaggressions. I felt singled out and cried racism even though those close to me advised to stop playing the race card.

I decided to get mental health support and met with a nurse-counsellor. "When you are being bullied, production goes down a lot, as much as 70 percent," the nurse told me. "Be gentle with yourself." She reassured me that I was not pretending to be mentally unwell.

Oftentimes we second-guess ourselves, question if we are being genuine when the effects of overt aggression and microaggressions hit us. Does this resonate with you or maybe you know someone who can relate? Regardless of the circumstances, I was not doing well. I was afraid of proving right those who assume—and sometimes outright audaciously claim—that "Africans aren't good enough." I had to be mentally tough to overcome the negativity and get back to normal so I could secure my job.

The nurse accurately predicted how the system would deal with me. Ms. Troller instructed my favourite senior manager to initiate a fact-finding investigation. Her efforts to recruit the front desk officer to lie about when I arrived at work and when I left the office were in vain. The officer was an ally. Nevertheless, I was hauled before a fact-finding committee for flying to Montréal during my mental health sick leave.

I had recognized that I was no longer safe to myself or to others when the "fierce fighter" part of me had been activated. I knew that leaving town was best for everybody. Ms. Troller had no idea what I might have done had I chosen to stay; if I had kept dragging myself to work. With that much anger bubbling inside—and knowing she was not only a bully, but also a racist—I knew I had to bring the temperature down. Her aggression reminded me of the British soldiers back home when I was young. I wanted to give her a thrashing! Unlike the soldiers, she had no gun. I might have beaten her thoroughly. It has taken me years to tame my "fierce fighter"; I hate it when I am pushed to the limit when "she" appears.

I imagined what would have happened had I stayed. They would have had a field day. "Look at that angry African woman. Fire her!" That is why I hopped on the plane and straight into the arms of my (now) husband, Sothemba, my safe space. He helped me as I coped with the stress; he was there for me when I needed the support the most.

Meanwhile, someone in Human Resources tried to trick me into denying that I had gone to Montréal. I told him I would not lie. If I had agreed, they would have nailed me as a liar, and that would have been grounds for dismissal. By suggesting that I lie, they miscalculated; my suspicion is that their action was based on the stereotype of a stupid and/or scared African.

He kept harassing me—even during my sick leave—at one point commanding me to report to the office immediately and sign some documents having to do with the hearing. As the nurse had advised, I sought support from the workers' union. A representative encouraged me to rest and try to diminish stress. When the hearing happened, the workers union representative sat with me throughout. Nothing happened to me. On the same day I was absolved of all charges, I was offered a new job!

My favourite senior manager and some staff members made a big show of sending me off. The manager made a moving farewell speech, appreciating my work. He was supposed to be an ally, but he had succumbed to the powerful Ms. Troller. Sadly, he had become part of the system that grieved me.

One thing is clear: hopping from one workplace to another cannot fix workplace racism because the system is inherently unjust. The unwritten societal hierarchy reigns supreme. It is a fact that society was, and still is, organized in ways that put whites first. Many social systems are not designed to support the oppressed even when it's well known, and often documented, that they are suffering. Studying systemic family counselling taught me that the problem is the problem, not the person. To fix the problem you have to fix the system, not the individual.

I remember a journalist asking me, if I had hard evidence against Ms. Troller. He wanted to publish an article exposing her. Hard evidence was the hurdle. When one is experiencing microaggressions there is usually little, if any, "hard evidence". Even so, Africans and other non-whites are asked, "How do you know? Can you *prove* it is racism?" In my situation, the community knew about Ms. Troller's reign of terror, but no one would hold her accountable because they feared her power. The system is rigged. It is inevitable that those who enjoy their privilege often do so without ever noticing the traces of racism in their language, their attitudes and behaviours.

These difficult stories are only snippets; there are more, including, happily, positive stories. I will also always remember the times—and there were more than a few— when I got to shine, when I felt the fulfilment of knowing I had made a difference. There are projects that have made me smile from ear to ear because my participation was valued and my contributions respected. What is true for all of us is that when we feel trusted, appreciated and safe, that is when we shine the most. Our mental health is not threatened when we are working in positive conditions. It has definitely been true for me.

As employees, we strive to find the "sweet spot" where our work and our purpose align and we feel fulfilled. When that alignment happens, we derive joy from serving and living purposeful lives. We do not need to be motivated by anyone to show up and serve as the best versions of ourselves. We go to work to be ourselves. When our value is recognized and our dignity is respected, our self-esteem needs are met.

As an African, it is my hope that all workplaces become safe for everyone to shine. A safe working environment is not only good for the worker's mind, body and soul, but it is good for their loved ones, too. They are the ones we steal so much time from in the service of making make their lives better.

We all have a role to play in creating safe and healthy work environments. I extend an invitation to everyone who works with other people to use these stories as conversation starters and mirrors to use for self-examination. We need to examine our inner lives to ensure that our words, attitudes, behaviours, and practices are in alignment and contribute to safe workplaces. We can begin by speaking truth to ourselves as we strive to be genuinely antiracist.

CHAPTER SIX

Dear Queen Elizabeth

It is 18 April, 2020. I jump out of bed, already angry. I had promised myself not to be quick to anger, but I have succumbed. It is Zimbabwe's Independence Day, the day British rule ended. Celebrate the good times! Really? Come on! Celebration? Not for me. I am boiling. Yet I open my balcony door and it is freezing cold. Minus 18 degrees Celsius. "Are my eyes playing tricks on me?" I wonder and mumble to myself, "What is it with the number 18?" I take a screenshot of my phone's home page displaying 18 April, and minus 18 degrees. The inside of my head is churning. "I am a tropical girl. Why am I here?" My forehead is furrowed and I feel pressure in the veins of both temples. I am freezing as I stand on the balcony of my apartment looking across to the Royal Canadian Legion pub and bar, here in the city of Iqaluit. There is a relentless squeezing sensation right in the middle of my head.

Flashes of memory come flooding out, one after the other: I am five again, gasping for breath. The British soldiers are striking my father and mother. I see blood. I hear groans. I am terrified and I cough incessantly. It is 45 years later, and the cough is still not gone! I see red. I have no one to talk to. I am breathing fire, my chest burning. It is visibly pumping up and down as I anxiously pace back and forth. Biting my nails, exaggerating the size of my eyes. Am I going crazy? What am I doing here? This is not the soil on which my umbilical cord is buried, yet my country is independent.

I go on WhatsApp and notice that my workout accountability group is on fire. I spot my cousin, Cathy, beautifully draped in the Zimbabwean flag; she looks gorgeous celebrating independence. I say to myself, "Instead of being angry about the troubles in Zimbabwe—all the social, economic, and political struggles my people are facing—why not copy Cathy? Why not dress up in the flag, own it, and have fun playing my mbira and healing on Facebook live?" That sounded like fun! I sprung into action.

Bright red lipstick, a bright face smiling back at my reflection. A stylish one-arm improvised Zimbabwean flag top and yellow shorts completed my outfit. Lights! Camera! (Facebook Live) Action! The sound of mbira is what I needed to hear. I play as if possessed. Then, unexpected words come. "Queen Elizabeth, is it too late to say you're sorry to that five-year-old child who witnessed her parents being brutalized by the British?"

I play "Nehondo" (Because of the War), a post liberation struggle song. It feels great to also call out the African leaders for not being true to the ideals of the struggle. I question why they appropriated the struggle for themselves and a few loyalists. I question how is it that Zimbabwe, a land of milk and honey, has so many of its children scattered all over the globe?

A question pops up in the comments. My sister Kiki from the US asks, "Why don't you just write off the Queen Elizabeth issue?" I tell her that people differ in terms of what they want for their healing. For some, vocalizing their pain is what's needed to finally put the matter to rest. It would be a great achievement for Her Royal Highness to actually address the consequences of the choices Britain made. It would be powerful and healing to acknowledge the costs, the impact on so many innocent children, and the damage to their parents' physical, spiritual, mental and psychological health.

When we genuinely apologize to those whose hearts we have wounded, they may heal faster. In the absence of our apologies, victims may remain stuck, wondering how to get past their trauma or hurt. How can anyone move forward if they don't have the resources to process trauma? Some never recover, dying from stress and anxiety. Some will pave their own path to forgiveness and healing. It may take a long time or it may go more quickly. Nevertheless, everyone must go through the process.

Years ago, I toyed with the idea of writing to the Queen. On Facebook Live that day I was not expecting to blurt out my secret need for her to issue a public apology. It just came out. I was trying to let bygones be bygones, as some Zimbabwean leaders had proposed. But I had given up after reading about how Kenyans were treated when they had asked for an apology. I did not want to get hurt, so I listened to the wisdom that we can heal from those who hurt us without actually getting any apology. Forgiveness is for our own benefit.

Perhaps because I was in Nunavut, where Prime Minister Trudeau had made an apology to Inuit, I felt my yearning for that kind of healing returning. Instead of pretending that I was over the pain completely, I decided that I would use the letter writing technique I learnt in my counselling training with Connect Zimbabwe. I reasoned that giving voice to the truth would be liberating for me, whether or not the Royal family ever even acknowledged my existence. I found an outlet for negative emotions that were taking me back to dark places I wished to never revisit. I wrote my way through my feelings.

> Dear Queen Elizabeth,
>
> Madam, I write today to share with you my childhood experiences during the liberation struggle in colonial Rhodesia. The woman I have become is very much influenced by my childhood experiences which have inspired me to work for racial equality.
>
> I realize I cannot change the past, neither can you, but I need to free myself by telling you my truth. I have overcome most of the victimhood and
>
> hypervigilance brought on by my childhood exposure to the violence, torture and trauma that my parents and other citizens suffered under the Rhodesian government. I decided to contact you once I realized that the reason for all this suffering was because the British, who granted the royal charter to colonize Zimbabwe, considered themselves racially superior to native Zimbabweans.
>
> One of the questions I have been asking myself is: "Is it too late for you to apologize to me, the five-year-old child?"
>
> We share a common identity as mothers. You know the love we have as mothers. It is that

love that I hope you will tap into as you read my request. I speak for myself, but I could also be speaking for millions who might be healed by your love.

Your voice as a mother, grandmother and great grandmother will have a lasting impact. Your empathy towards the mothers visited by the brutality of war at their doorstep, would help to stop racial injustice and avoidable wars. As I aspire to bring mothers together to collectively heal the world through teaching our children love, I am convinced that is it only through being vulnerable and telling the truth—without shame or blame, just facing facts—that we can show our children the way to loving one another unconditionally.

In the wake of the damage racism has inflicted on humanity, especially to Africans and Afro-descendants, the unconditional love of a mother will go a long way to make things right. That, and treating those impacted as if they were your own children, grandchildren and great grandchildren.

Today, as you sit on the throne as one of the world's most powerful matriarchs, I invite you to join me in this cause.

It is no longer just for me that I make this bold request. It is for the future, for our children and their children and grandchildren, to know that we worked for racial equality. We never want to see another human being suffer simply because others feel racially superior and enjoy privileges, while those deemed inferior experience systemic racism and multiple poverties.

It is scary to admit that an apology from you is what I need; yet it feels right. We are afraid to speak the truth because we fear people in power. For the longest time, I kept saying I needed the royal family to realize the importance of making things right to the children of war, and to change the world through the spirit of true reconciliation.

Today is Independence Day, the day the British said to Zimbabwe, "You can now rule yourselves." I summoned all my courage to address you on this special day. No one has ever said, "Sorry," to the children and their mothers and their fathers, for the trauma they endured under British rule.

Your Majesty, we are imprisoned in our so-called independence because there never has been freedom for the children born before and after the struggle. We reel in the aftermath of a colonial legacy where real wealth was in the hands of a few and the majority wallowed in poverty. It has grown worse, but that is not to say there are no good people in Africa. Just that the system of police brutality and violence has never stopped, and the poverty of the majority and the riches of a few, as Ngugi WaThiongo puts it, continues.

Hear the plea of a girl who not just witnessed violence but also experienced violence in her first decade of life. Today, four decades later and the mother of three adults who hope to thrive, despite living in a world full of hate against them simply because of the colour of their skin, I am hopeful. I am hopeful that you will grant me my childhood wish and heal not only *my* wound but that of millions hurt by the British Army's acts of abuse and cruelty.

May you be blessed.

Yours Truly,
Francisca Ndaiziweyi Mandeya

While I did not end up sending this letter, I hope the Queen will get to know about it from this book.
I am not a victim. I am a victor. Mental illness has threatened to take root in me as I have tried to contain all the worries I carry in my head—from my personal life to global issues. I make use of the tools I have to liberate myself. Letter writing is one tool among many in my self-help toolbox.
In spite of all we know to be true, I still find myself fascinated and attracted to the royal family. I watched the wedding of Harry and his love Meghan as they showed the world that love transcends human-made racial barriers. On March 7, 2021, my 51st birthday, I watched Prince Harry and his wife, Duchess Meghan, bare their souls in an interview with Oprah Winfrey. Try as they might to have seen love transcend human-made racial barriers, they revealed the ugly truth that societal racism—including inside the royal family—still persists.
Their courage to speak truth to power emboldened me as I sat anxiously wondering about my decision to write my truth to the

Queen. The feelings I experienced simply *anticipating* backlash from those blindly loyal to the monarchy were scary. Yet, like the brave royal couple, I realized I must not fear speaking my truth; it is the only way transformation can happen. I felt more connected and empathetic to Harry and Meghan, especially considering how racism can attack one's mental health, not to mention confronting those closest to us: our families. Their speaking out affirmed my conviction that standing in our authentic truth liberates us. There is however, a price for standing up for what one believes is right and just.

Another member of the royal family who inspired me through her authenticity was Princess Diana, Prince Harry's mother. She was a darling to me and many other Zimbabweans. She was beautiful, and I do not know a single person who did not love her. Her down-to-earth ways stirred our hearts. When Princess Diana visited my native land, she refused to be deceived by politicians who wanted her to believe that all was well and clean in Zimbabwe. She refused to be escorted to the pleasant looking parts of Harare. On her own, she organized a visit to the poor, sitting on the ground playing "draughts" (what some call checkers) with ordinary people in Mbare. She wanted to see real people and their real struggles. Princess Diana did not like war and was bold in her actions to oppose it, working to clear landmines from post-war zones. Perhaps that is what made me even love her more.

All the work I have done to open my heart has released me from the pain of my past. I will never let victimhood or hypervigilance steal my peace. The past cannot imprison me; it can only teach me. The past cannot imprison you; it can only teach you. The past cannot imprison us; it can only teach us.

CHAPTER SEVEN

Being "Black" in North America

"It's true that for me, a part of being Black on this side of the world has been about constantly grieving the deaths of people I've never met.

—*Yamri Tadesse
(Excerpt from a 2017 essay for the Canadian Broadcasting Company)*

I remember being so excited when Denis Lambe of the Royal Canadian Mounted Police (RCMP) extended an invitation for me to be in dialogue with Iqaluit RCMP officers. It was diversity week, and my presentation was on how Black people want to be treated by the police. I did not prepare a script. I opted to flow from the heart.

"We are so diverse in our "Blackness" that I cannot speak on behalf of the community here in Iqaluit," I began. "There are more than ten African countries represented here; and there are Afro-Caribbeans from the islands, too. Culturally, we are very different. Even my sister here, born of the same parents and sharing the same birthday, is different from me in terms of her preferences. However, one common African value is "Ubuntu"—"I am because you are." So, in terms of treatment, I would say that we just want to be treated equally, fairly, and with dignity like any other human being."

After completing the presentation, I shared my culture with the officers. They say culture is what you eat so I brought sadza (a Zimbabwean staple made from maize) and stewed tilapia. As my thumbs plucked at the blades of the mbira and song-stories of joy and pain poured from my heart, I noticed some eyes closing, smiles widening, and tears forming. The music was speaking to their souls. Even the tips of my feet registered the joy I felt. I will always be grateful for any police officers who show a human face when dealing with other human beings.

Historically, I learnt that Inuit have difficulty trusting police because their livelihoods had been destroyed and they were forced into settlements; this is much like what happened in Africa. The intentional slaying of sled dogs and forcing children to attend residential schools were gross violations of Inuit rights. I know that work is being done to mend relations; my hope is that justice will prevail.

Personally, I have only had positive experiences with the police in Iqaluit. In 2019, during the annual international 16 Days of Activism protesting gender-based violence, there was a march from the Royal Bank of Canada to Nunnata Sunakkutaangit Museum. I marched side by side with a thoughtful white police officer. We had a respectful, meaningful conversation about equity, and I told him about my gender equality book, *Mother Behold Thy Son*. He shared that he had been raised by a single mother who had instilled in him the message to treat women as equals. He kept checking with me to see how I was doing. "I am fine. It's just so freezing cold", I answered halfway through the march. It was minus 22 Celsius. He dipped into his pocket and gave me hand warmers. His kindness will always have a place in my heart.

Ever since I arrived in North America, watching the news often brought tears to my eyes as I realized how often people who look like me were being killed in our neighbouring country, the United States. One might ask, "Why would you concern yourself with your neighbour's problems?" Well, because the murdered people all inhabited brown bodies like mine, and I feel the pain of injustice done to them simply because of the way they looked. Yes, they may not now be from Africa, it's worse; they were *stolen* from Africa. We are one. It might as well be me.

I realize that my sister and I were constantly traumatized as we watched person after person—people who looked like us—being murdered. For the most part the killers were white men, often police officers. We were caught in a web of trauma and vicarious trauma. To protect my heart, I decided to stop watching television.

Social media had the last laugh at my attempt to run away from televised racial violence. My heart was not protected as I watched Derrick Chauvin squeeze the life out of George Floyd in 2020. I mourned inconsolably. His lament, "I can't breathe" haunted me. Of all the murders of African Americans I had seen on television, this one ripped me apart. As he called out, "Mama", and breathed his last breath, my head was spinning, my whole face hot; I felt as if I was going through open heart surgery without anesthesia.

What mother or father would ever want their child to die that way? The heartache of a mother losing a son gripped me. I did not have to be George Floyd's mother to feel my womb contracting in pain over the loss of a son.

Any mother who has gone through labour and who has lost a child knows that pain. As I experienced the pain of his mother in my body, I researched and found out that his mother was already in heaven. Whoa! He had been calling out for his mother, but she was already gone. He had a child. He had an aunt. He had siblings. And there were all of us—his unknown sisters and brothers—crying for him, too.

The white police officer who brutally murdered George Floyd—sentenced to more than 22 years in prison—triggered memories of the white men who had brutalized my father and mother while I watched, 45 years ago. I was overcome with feeling. I'd been emotionally hijacked! I went into a dark place I had vowed never to visit, but this tragedy was too much. It hit without warning.

I thought of the words of Yamri Taddese, the Ethiopian-Canadian journalist whose words I have adopted: "It's true that for me, a part of being Black on this side of the world has been about constantly grieving the deaths of people I've never met after they had become a hashtag, [among them in the US: Ahmaud Arbery, Sandra Bland, Michael Brown, Rayshard Brooks, Philando Castile, Eric Garner, Elijah McClain, Tamir Rice, Daunte Wright and, in Canada, Andrew Loku. And so many others, whose deaths I mourn still. Each time a video of police killing a Black person surfaces online, I'm caught in the see-saw of anger and heartache." I, too, was also going up and down in a seesaw of anger and heartache. Why? "*How can?*" (as my paternal grandmother, Mbuya Mandeya, would say in her evocative broken English.)

The heartache of being African and knowing we are at the bottom rung of the race ladder, and therefore not viewed as equals by most of the world, was real. Footage showing Africans in the Chinese city of Guangzhou (Canton) being blamed, beaten and harassed for causing the coronavirus, did not make the pain any better. That is why such murders could happen repeatedly and Derrick Chauvin, the murderer in the George Floyd case, could be so coldblooded and unrepentant. It sent a clear message to all of us. Racism against Black people is real. Their message: "Your lives do not matter." Our emphatic reply: "But they do!"

Black Lives Matter

"Black Lives Matter!" Those were the words on my hand-made sign as I joined thousands of marchers to protest police violence in the United States and Canada, too—even though police behaviour in the two countries are not comparable. With my sign leaning by my front door, I put on black lipstick, exaggerated the colour of my eyebrows, and put more eyeliner and mascara than ever before. I set aside my loathing for being identified as "Black." This issue was too important. That day I was ready for the "Black look."

I wore my black and white headdress, the Zebra print to show my indigenous identity, my totem, and to make a statement about my race. I wore dramatic black shades to complete the desired look. I did not have a suitable black jacket, so I settled for my maroon one, tan boots and white mittens with bead designs (designed by an Inuk woman) that remind me of Africa. Fashion police might have arrested me! Did I care? No. I went live on Facebook telling my friends where I was and why I was doing what I was doing. I took a picture with Alassua Hanson, a young Inuk woman whose sign read, "My Skin Colour is Not a Threat." I chuckled as I noticed that she was a much lighter brown than me. You will find our picture at the end of this chapter.

Our colonial histories of racial injustice brought us together, a history that says our lives are expendable, valued less than others deemed of "better racial stock." Today, Inuit were our allies, acknowledging that people like me faced disproportionate discrimination. Other allies who normally do not go to racial injustice protests joined in solidarity. We tend to be polarized and forget to embrace those who empathize with us. I embraced many, I felt the love.

In the tragedy of Black people being killed, I saw the opportunity for humanity to unite in ways we had not done before. While I appreciated the love I was receiving, sadly, in other circles hate, arrogance and ignorance were also playing out. Walls have ears. It hurt to learn that some respected leaders were stereotyping Black people as a homogenous, violent bunch. They feared that we would destroy property, as a minority of protestors who looked like us had done in the US. I thought about how important it is to acknowledge our anger, to be righteously angry, but to *never* act while in the throes of being hijacked by those feelings. Damaging property would be self-sabotaging. We were not going to follow that route.

Those who stereotyped us in Iqaluit spoke from a position of privilege, being on a higher rung of the race ladder. Their false consciousness and hyperrational arrogance made them label us "those people", a common phrase many use to demean us as less than, the "other." Ironically, subsequent investigations—with verifiable video footage—revealed that some of the property damage in the US had been the work of white supremacists.

We tend to judge and prejudge people, to draw conclusions about who they are and how they behave based on their assigned race. We condemn without evidence. Have you ever judged, or have you been judged that way? Racial profiling paints with one broad brush. The result? Perpetuating injustice. Those who judge do so without looking at each person as an individual with unique characteristics. For African people, it is like losing the race before it has even begun. It does not matter how good a person you are. If you have experienced this yourself, know you are not alone.

I was not alone as the multicultural crowd swelled at the four corners, the busiest intersection in Iqaluit. People kept coming, despite concerns about the coronavirus. To be honest, fear of the pandemic was subordinate to the fear of an ongoing, lifelong racial injustice pandemic.

The march was the largest in recent history. Some people wore masks; some did not. Nunavut was living in its own bubble without a single Covid-19 case. As we occupied the four corners in the city centre, I noticed Dadi, my sister from Zimbabwe, approaching. She stood next to me. Jordana, a sister from one of the Caribbean islands, was behind me. A hand encircled me and soothed my back as I silently cried. It was Alicia, another sister, from Nova Scotia. Our sisterhood in grief brought us together; it knew no geography. All these sisters' faces carrying stories of pain.

It was apparent that the grief we were experiencing was not only for George Floyd, but represented the compounded grief for all people of our kind who have been killed by other human beings who see us as lesser beings. Whenever I try to understand why we are treated this way, I turn to the history of slavery and colonization, to liberation struggles, and to my current post-independence reality. It was so much to carry, to remember.

My head felt as if it was exploding; my chest was heavy. I was suffocating. There was no air. I might have been on the verge of a panic attack. Just then, the words "I can't breathe" escaped my mouth. I could not stand the deathly silence. It reminded me of the soldiers silencing us. We could not cry even though I wanted to cry; I *needed* to cry.

Suddenly, I began shouting, crying, beseeching over and over, "I can't breathe. I can't breathe. I can't breathe. I can't breathe. I can't breathe." People were quiet. Feeling alone in the silence, I managed to add a shaky invitation, calling out, "Join me!" After a moment, I heard the crowd's collective voice growing louder. They were chanting with me: "I can't breathe!" Dadi was screaming, "I can't breathe" and crying so hard that I began crying, too. I rubbed her back, while Alicia rubbed mine. I needed release. We could not wait for instructions from a march organizer, Clayton, or other organizers. I, we, all of us, had such an urgent need to pour out our grief. I needed to save myself there and then from losing my mind.

As the chanting began, I felt complete and went quiet. The crowd quieted, too; their voices moving from angry cries to mournful murmurs and then, at last, stillness. We, the people, had set the tone and now our peaceful protest could commence.

We marched along Queen Elizabeth II Way where I spotted my sister, Tina, and Tafy, Dadi's little sister. Tina's handmade sign struck a chord: "Get your knee off our necks." Similar strong, in-your-face messages were written on many signs. Tina's face was stained as a river of tears streamed down her cheeks. She looked so vulnerable, the salt from her drying tears mixing with the dust from the street. I wished I could hug her. Making eye contact with her triggered so much pain in my heart; a fresh torrent of tears poured out.

Our unspoken pain connected us as we arrived at the legislative assembly where Clayton, a lead organizer, spoke. He respectfully, but emphatically, called on the powers that be to hear the plight of Black people in Nunavut. The march resumed and we made our final stop at the RCMP building.

Clayton spoke against police brutality; another organizer, Jukipa, a young Inuk woman, spoke in solidarity. Clayton then invited any of us in the crowd to speak. Lesedi, an eight-year-old girl told the crowd, "I should not be here. I should be playing with my friends." Many of us cried as she shared stories of experiencing racism at school.

I had no intention of speaking but the pain in my heart propelled my feet forward. Before I knew it, I was headed toward the stage. I was not sure what I would say, but I sensed that speaking would help me, and maybe others. As I faced the crowd, I did not realize how big it was. A voice inside said, "Let the heart lead."

I started with a question: "Who chose to be born the way they look? Raise your hand." No one did.

"No one right!?," I said, continuing, "What crime did we commit being born the way we are?" The crowd replied as one: "None." I asked another question: "Does anybody here want to be treated like Black people the world over are treated? Raise your hand." No one did.

"Why not?" I asked. "Because it sucks!" someone in the crowd called out. "Because it sucks; it's painful," I agreed.

I kept going. I could feel something moving inside of me, guiding my words. "I don't know for how long we have kept quiet. We kept telling them intersectional analysis does not do us justice. The world over, from the superpowers to the less powerful, they all agree on how Black people are treated: on the colour ladder, we are on the bottom rung. Indeed, I was called "nigger" for the first time, here in Canada. I did not know I was a nigger. It was a seven or eight-year-old who called me that.

"When it comes to language, sometimes I do not like being called Black. There is a journalist among us who wanted to interview me during Black history month. It is the only month we have a voice here in North America and he wanted to talk to a "Black" person. I stopped him. 'I actually don't like being called Black.' I am sorry to the Black people who are attached to the label, but that is where the lie begins, right?"

Then I asked the crowd, "What's my skin colour? The crowd called out, 'Brown.' I repeated, "What colour is it?" Again they replied, 'Brown.' I nodded. I concluded with, "So, if it's skin colour, let's be correct about it because "black" is mischievous; "white" is mischievous. If and when we begin to talk about race, let's call things by their proper names. We did not choose to be born the way we are; let's all love one another. Let's do away with the love of power and focus on the power of love."

After me, others spoke their minds, expressing the pain they felt. One of them, Rowena spoke with raw honestly. "My name is Rowena. I am not a nigger. Call me Rowena." After the march, she told me her daughter had asked her, "Mom, don't you think that was too much (saying "nigger" out loud?) Ro answered, "That's what they call us, so why shy away from it? They know we have names." After the march, I went on Facebook and posted:

Qujannamiik (Thank you) to everyone who came. Today was beautiful and painful. We kneeled in discomfort. Different colours, we were one. Sitting in the discomfort of racial injustices ignored for far too long. It is time to Wake Up, Wise Up and Rise Up! Mothers, we have work to do. We sure can teach love. In *Mother Behold Thy Son*, I wrote: "I am a child of the universe, seeking to live a full life, a life of abundance, a life of equality. I am both student and teacher. I stand for my full freedom. I am committed to freeing myself from the boxes of gender, race, religion and class that society tries to trap all of us in, threatening to silence us and denying us our full humanity." I am haunted by George Floyd's call for help to his mother.

I wrote *Mother Behold Thy Son* in 2019. To behold means to admire. Every mother longs for that. I am still processing the pain of mothers who can no longer behold their sons, because another son took their lives. The system took their sons. Am I afraid for my son? Yes, but I am also afraid for other mothers' sons—those that look like mine and also those that don't.

For a long time, the pain of Black mothers has not been recognized. The picture of a pregnant African American mother which had a sign that read, "We do not carry for 9 months and struggle in labour for 9 hours, just for you to kneel on our necks for 9 minutes! Black Lives Matter", gripped the core of my heart and womb. You will find the picture at the end of this chapter.

To all mothers, please recognize that we have been called—called to stand up; called to speak up; called to act. We are love. We are hope. We are comfort. I pray that our sons will never be hunted again. Work for love. Work for freedom. Work for racial equality.

After a heavy sharing, it is important not to leave people on a low note. So I went live on Facebook with my mbira, my go to instrument, and played and sang as if a spirit had gripped me. Fadhili Junior, a friend and brother from Kenya, commented that he felt goose bumps as I sang. I was inviting the Spirit to heal us—the Holy Spirit, the Spirit of Africa, the Spirit of our ancestors. I composed that song to help me deal with the loss of George Floyd.

I am a life giver; I long to behold my children treating all human beings with love. I am a fighter for peace. If we want peace we must fight for justice; if we want justice we must speak truth; if we speak truth, we must begin by telling it to ourselves. It begins with you and me.

The next day I received a WhatsApp message from an Inuk friend who prefers to remain anonymous. "I attended [the protest] yesterday with my son. Thank you for speaking. My son and I listened to you and all the others who spoke. It has started a good discussion in our little family. I will try to raise anti-racist children."

It was heart-warming to know that my voice had made a difference. Our collective voice made a difference. Our voice is not just meant for us. It touches others who might be inspired to take action and make the world a much better place. Your voice matters; my voice matters. *Our* voices matter.

The author, right, with Alassua Hanson, at the George Floyd demonstration in Iqaluit, the capital city of the Canadian territory of Nunavut. Photo: Unknown

A mother of two African American sons expressing herself at a protest over the murder of George Floyd.
Photo: Thema McClain

CHAPTER EIGHT

My "Cousin" Jane Elliot

Get over the fact that you are white. There is one race, the human race.

—*Jane Elliot, US diversity educator*

Hearing one of my mentors, Jane Elliot, say, "I am not a white woman, I am a faded black person", made me smile. Her denial of her assigned colour spoke to me since I also deny my assigned colour. Long before I was born, Jane Elliot had been teaching anti-racism education. I was drawn to her; I wanted to sit at her feet and learn.

Learning is a lifelong process to which I must always be open. *Un*learning is another lifelong process necessary for transformation. *Re*learning is also the same. I am open. Are you?

With my eyes glued to the screen, I watched a short video clip introducing Jane Elliot's pedagogy. It landed powerfully on my heart. I felt connected to the naked truth she was sharing. There was no need to dilute it, to sugar coat it. It was uncomfortable, but who said transformation is comfortable? Here's a little of what she said:

> I want every white person in this room who would be happy to receive the same treatment that our Black citizens endure in this society, please stand. (Pause.) Nobody is standing. That says very plainly that you know what's happening; you know you *don't* want it for you. I wanna know why you are so willing to accept it, or to allow it to happen, for others?

There is no thing such as an innocent bystander. We are either racist or antiracist. Jane Elliot's fierce spirit spoke to mine. I was excited to know that there are people who do not look like me who feel the pain of racial injustice; people who don't just speak about it but actively work on dismantling the system that created and perpetuates it.

Jane Elliott's disruptive pedagogy forces people who identify as white to face race issues truthfully and to confront their biases. The only issue I would challenge her to reconsider in her teaching is language. It matters. The terms "black" and "white" represent political language. Giving both blackness and whiteness (which was invented by the stroke of a pen) power perpetuates the race binary and is, in my opinion, problematic. Race is a lie.

We must be prepared to tell the truth. Paulo Freire, author of *Pedagogy of the Oppressed*, was right when he said, "To say a true word is to transform the world." He taught that truth has two parts, reflection and action. If we only speak a phrase such as "racial equality", that is verbalism. And, if we only act without reflecting on racial equality, that is activism. Activism alone will not make the problem go away. Radical action that attacks the *root* is what is necessary to foster lasting change. To be true is to do both, to reflect and act.

I do not know how many times I watched the video, but I was as happy as "a little puppy at a wedding" as they say back home in Zimbabwe. Tail-wagging sideways, jumping-up-and-down happiness. How could I have missed knowing about this kind of transformational teacher, *my* kind of teacher? When she said, "We are cousins" and shook hands with Jada Pinkett Smith and her crew on Jada's Red Table Talk television program, love flooded more than my heart; my whole chest was engulfed in its warmth. We *are* all cousins. Let that sink in.

"There is one race", the human race, Ms. Elliott said, and "the human race began with black women." That message has been reiterated by many including John Biewen, a journalist and Duke University documentarian. In his 2019 Ted Talk, "The Lie That Invented Racism", he noted:

> Science is clear; we are one human race, we're all related, all descended from a common ancestor in Africa. Some people walked out of Africa into colder, darker places and lost a lot of their melanin. Some of us more than others, but genetically we are all 99.9 percent the same. There is no gene for whiteness or blackness or Asianness or what have you."

It's odd to me that we talk of "people of colour" as if there are people of *no* colour. We all have skin colour, but we lie about its correctness or accuracy. We need to open our eyes to see the truth. What is *your* true colour? What are *our* true colours?

My first time recognizing that notions of race are a lie was in 2006 at the Grail (retreat) Centre in South Africa. It's where I learnt that race, like gender, is socially constructed. My eyes were opened, and I have never been the same since. Being female and African, I understood how these socially constructed barriers to humanity intersected to stifle my voice and deny me my full humanity.

I learnt about Rosa Parks, legendary US civil rights activist who refused to acknowledge white privilege and move to the back of a city bus. Her act of civil disobedience triggered the Montgomery, Alabama bus boycott, a historic moment in advancing the rights of African Americans in the US.

With this knowledge planted securely inside of me, I was hungry to raise my consciousness more, to get answers to the deep questions I had not only about why human beings treated other people like me so badly, but also why Africa was poor. I have read Freire's *Pedagogy of the Oppressed* and *Education for Critical Consciousness;* ditto Frantz Fanon's *The Wretched of the Earth* and *Black Skin White Masks*. Also, the work of murdered South African anti-apartheid leader, Steve Biko, including *I Write What I Like*. My hope lies in the belief that if race has been constructed it can be deconstructed.

Freirean pedagogy teaches us to examine the entirety of the political, economic and social circumstances that create a culture of silence. Jane Elliot's approach poses problems to provoke our emotions, forcing us to deeply reflect *and* to act to change our undesired reality.

In an appearance on Red Table Talk, Jane Elliot shared that the notion of race started during the Spanish Inquisition that began in 1478. Here is a relevant part of John Biewen's November 2019 TED talk on that point:

> Gomes Eanes de Zurara a Portuguese man, wrote a book in the 1450s in which he did something that no one had ever done before, according to Dr. [Ibram X.] Kendi, [author of *How to be an Antiracist.*] He lumped together *all* the people of Africa, a vast, diverse continent, and he described them as a distinct group, inferior and beastly. Never mind that in that precolonial time, some of the most sophisticated cultures in the world were in Africa. Why would this guy make this claim? Turns out it helps to follow the money.

First of all, [Gomes Eanes de Zurara] was hired to write that book by the Portuguese king and, just a few years before, slave traders. Here we go, slave traders tied to the Portuguese crown had effectively pioneered the Atlantic slave trade; they were the first Europeans to sail directly to sub-Saharan Africa to kidnap and enslave African people. So, it was suddenly really helpful to have a story about the inferiority of African people to justify this new trade to other people, to the church, to themselves. And with the stroke of a pen, Gomes Eanes de Zurara invented both blackness and whiteness because he basically created the notion of blackness through this description of Africans and, as Dr. Kendi says, blackness has no meaning without whiteness. Other European countries followed the Portuguese lead in looking to Africa for human property and free labor, and in adopting this fiction about the inferiority of

African people. Racism didn't start with a misunderstanding; it started with a lie.

> So, dear "cousins"—sister and brother human relatives—with that said, I invite you to get over the "fact" that there are white or Black people. There is one race, the human race. I thank my "cousin" Jane Elliot for being such a teacher, and John Biewen for recognizing how the media is complicit in perpetuating racial inequality. I also applaud citizen journalists who are pointing their cameras to show the world the truth. (A special shout out to then 17-year-old Darnella Frazier, who filmed the murder of George Floyd. The Pulitzer Prize board awarded her with a special citation in June 2021, noting the crucial role citizens can play in journalists' quest for truth and justice.)

Lies must not win; truth must win. Hate must not win; love must win. It always does. It begins with our being open to it, acknowledging our part in sustaining it, owning it, and then engaging in transformative action. Once he learned the truth about the lie that invented racism, John Biewen transformed himself. What will you do?

CHAPTER NINE

To Educate or Indoctrinate: That is the Question

One of the 17 United Nations sustainable development goals is ensuring a quality education. In his paper, "What Makes a Curriculum?", Phillip Stabback believes that education must be inclusive, equitable, characterized by quality learning, promoting lifelong education and, he notes, it must be relevant to holistic development.

Education and development are indeed two sides of the same coin, as Sally Timmel and Anne Hope, my Training for Transformation tutors taught me. I grew up hearing that education is the gateway to success. For me, the question is,

Are we teaching or indoctrinating? And, when it comes to race, how is our education system doing? What are we teaching our children? Does our education and socialization of our children provide the gateway for success? Does it teach them to treat other human beings as equals, to see them as fully human?

Parents are undeniably children's first teachers and, in the case of mothers, instruction begins in the womb. You might want to pause and reflect on the role your mother, father, or a person who may have taken their place, played in who you have become. What do you remember them teaching you?

Teachers, what type of education are you providing? When I say "teachers" I mean any of us who are educating our children, and who serve as educators in our communities and the world. We must teach critical consciousness guided by unconditional love, and we must ensure that our teaching cultivates curiosity and rejects indoctrination.

"Schools do not want people to know the truth," educator Jane Elliott reminds us. "We teach Black history as if it started during slavery", adding that children from 5 to 18 are indoctrinated with lies that perpetuate white supremacy. She says it is unacceptable—and absurd—to teach that Christopher Columbus "discovered" America and expect racial equality to become a reality. My school curriculum in Zimbabwe taught me that David Livingstone "discovered" Victoria Falls, yet the Tonga people had lived by them for centuries (just as the Native Americans had been on land that became the United States for centuries as well.)

White supremacy was one of the ideologies of colonial Zimbabwe, then known as Rhodesia. In dialogue with a mother in my inner circle, Zvi, who is raising children in the US, she shared her need to re-educate them. The genocide of Native Americans was erased from the narrative, replaced with some fantastic "happy ending" pilgrimage, she said. Such "history" is the enemy of truth. Zvi and her children do not celebrate Columbus Day or Christopher Columbus; it is just a day out of school. To celebrate him like a hero would send the message that what he did was right and just. Her children now know the truth and that helps them to understand and have compassion for Native Americans, especially since they still suffer intergenerational trauma and experience racial injustice.

In my book, *Mother Behold Thy Son*, I shared how my sister Jo corrected her son for perpetuating gender stereotypes. She was surprised to hear him dissing pink as a "silly" colour only meant for girls. She corrected him there and then! She realized she had to pay more attention to where he was picking up life lessons. As a mother, her child's first teacher, she had to *re*-educate her son. Similarly, when it comes to race, we must be attentive to what our children are being exposed to, committing ourselves to countering any false notions they may be developing.

Telling the truth to children—and correcting revisionist history, uncomfortable as it may be—is the only way to fight mind control. Replace "*my*" truth with "*the* truth" to avoid half-truths. It is sad that too often teachers, parents, and guardians are at odds with each other because those differences are confusing for children and make learning harder.

When it comes to race, we must not equivocate. To unmask white lies and black lies, we need to open our eyes, see the truth, tell it, teach it, live it. We are all equal; unique but equal.

Talking about eyes and equality, Jane Elliot performed her now famous blue and brown eyes experiment for the first time on April 5, 1968, the day after Martin Luther King, Jr. was assassinated. In light of what had happened, she revised her lesson plan, creating for her third-grade students a lived experience of discrimination. (Education must be relevant, another of Freire's principles). An educator seizes teachable moments to help address real-life challenges.

Jane Elliot divided the class into those with blue eyes and those with brown. She bestowed privileges to one group and denied them to the other. Over three days (including switching which group was deemed superior), her students directly experienced being the prized, dominant group and the shunned, subordinate one. This kind of education teaches from the head *and* from the heart. It is from there that the desire for change comes.

The experiment wasn't appreciated in some circles. "I didn't know how this exercise would work. If I had known how it would work, I probably wouldn't have done it," Ms. Elliott told the *New York Times* years later. "If I had known that our four children would be spit on and their belongings would be destroyed, that they would be verbally and physically abused by their peers, by their teachers, and some of the parents of their peers, because they had what that community labeled as a Nigger-lover for a mother", she says she would have had second thoughts. Ms. Elliott's children weren't the only family members to face consequences. Her parents lost their restaurant business after widespread boycotts; her husband was isolated from his friend group, and Ms. Elliott was shunned by many teachers in her school system. Still, she has no regrets.

Jane Elliott is 88 now and says she has no plans to step back from educating people—not until every living person understands that the problem underlying racism in America is easy to identify and fix. "Just stop believing that there's more than one race. Realize that we're all members of the same race. That's the human race," Ms. Elliott says. "Every person on the face of the earth is my 30th to 50th cousin. I get really angry at my pale-faced cousins when they abuse my cousins of other color groups, because of pale-faced people's ignorance about skin color."

We must all be conscious enough to know that "no education is neutral." Whatever we are taught serves a purpose. It is one of Paulo Freire's core principles. According to Freire, education does two things, it either liberates us, or it domesticates us to the status quo, to support the existing order. Jane Elliot's way of teaching not only challenges racial inequality, but also invites participants to challenge social norms. I invite *you* to use these tools to be bold and courageous.

Many of us are afraid of what people will say if we stand in our truth. We fear rejection, harm, ridicule. What sacrifices are we prepared to make for our children and for others so that justice and racial equality can become a reality?

My belief in the possibility of racial equality is unwavering. I am not that crazy for thinking it is possible. I have power as a mother, a teacher, my children's first teacher. And, someday, I hope to stand with my daughters and son as they have (and teach) their own children. What position and power do you have? How are you using it?

CHAPTER TEN

Swimming is a White Sport

The sad thing is most of the hate was coming from adults. As kids we were just being competitive. Nobody was racist until they were taught by their parents.
—Zanele Danisa Mtomba, the author's daughter, commenting on swimming competitions with whites

In 2002, my two daughters Nomalanga and Zanele, got a national ranking in swimming at age 10 and 9 respectively, much to the ire of many who could not stomach the fact that African girls can swim competitively.

An angry mom whom I will call Mrs. Rhodes, could be heard cursing her daughter who I will call Sally: "How could you finish behind "that black thing?" By "that black thing", she meant my nine-year-old daughter, Zanele (Za). She had just swum faster than anyone else in her age group, provoking Mrs. Rhodes' ire.

As children, most of us revere our mothers. What mother says is right and it is obeyed. The moment Mrs. Rhodes said "that black thing", she taught her child racism. Sally could no longer see Za as an equal competitor but, instead, as a lesser being, a "black thing." Mrs. Rhodes created that experience for both her daughter and mine. In that one phrase, she killed the confidence and spirit of a child who had overcome hydrophobia to become an amazing swimmer. At the same time, she planted the seeds of racism in her own daughter's heart.

My beautiful dark chocolate Zanele was frantically trying to make eye contact with me; she beckoned me to come close. She was wearing her maroon swimsuit as she prepared for her next race. Her big brown eyes were brimming with tears. The pain she felt pierced my heart. She looked like she had seen a ghost. "Mommy, I don't want to swim anymore. They are calling me a 'black thing', and saying nasty things. They're threatening me," she cried.

"Who is "they" Za?", I asked.

"Mrs. Rhodes is mad at me for swimming faster than Sally," she said. "They are both talking about me as if I am not there, pointing at me and saying, "that black thing."

The squeezing in my chest and the burning in my gut riled me. God, is it not enough? Zanele means enough, Lord. It *is* enough now! My thoughts were racing. I was panting as if I had just finished a 100-metre dash. This was too much. Not after everything we had gone through to get to the meet. I was supposed to be cheering my daughters like any other African parent—shouting and cheering at the top of her voice. I was not prepared for another heartbreak. I held back my tears and spoke with as much calm as I could muster.

"Za, we came all the way from Marondera, riding in a *gonyet* at almost midnight," I began. (Gonyet is a Zimbabwean term for long haul trucks.) "We bought a new swimming costume to make sure you would comply with the rules. Now you want to give up after all the effort it took to get here?! No, Zanele! Whose daughter are you?"

"Yours, Mommy," she replied, her voice a little stronger.

"Okay. Go and tell the girls: "I am a dolphin, I will outswim you again!" I encouraged her, "Remember our journey and why you wanted to come. You are beautiful and you are strong. Do not fear anyone, Za. Don't give them power. They are afraid of your talent. Show them."

"Okay, Mommy", she said, sauntering off, a half-smile on her lips and a sparkle in her eyes. She swam her heart out and did her best. She won some and she lost some. When she was done, she shared that the girls on her team were at it again, putting her down. I lost it! I wanted to retaliate. I struggled to control myself; the fighter in me badly wanted to go after the white parent and her child and strike back with a racist jab, "That's why your (white) farms are being invaded by Zanu PF! " I wanted to say. (Zanu PF is the Zimbabwean African National Union-Patriotic Front, the country's ruling party which took power after the country achieved independence).

I am happy that I stopped myself, otherwise "Mrs. Rhodes" might have succeeded in luring me into a duel of who could say the most racist thing. Most of the so-called white swim competition parents were rich farmers or corporate managers. The parent who attacked my daughter—and the girls who were swimming with her—opened wounds I thought had healed long ago. I couldn't have been more wrong.

The memories of my country's liberation struggle came alive in me. Many white people in Zimbabwe were still practicing racial discrimination even though we were said to be independent. Despite being free, the white farmers still owned the land some of which they or their forefathers had forcefully taken. They still thought of themselves as Rhodesian. My brother and sister Zimbabweans, the rightful owners of the land, were told to "let bygones be bygones" and to live peacefully with the whites.

Living in peace was a sham. High-level deals were made between those with political power and those with economic power. The whites remained rich and superior, even in an independent Zimbabwe. It was only when politicians were desperate to retain political power that they used reclaiming stolen land to entice non-whites to support them. The whites recognized they were no longer safe on the appropriated land. In this context, an activity like swimming was still understood to be a "white" sport. I have said before and repeat now: When systemic injustice—in this case, blatant racism—is not pulled out at the root, it will continue to grow.

I had no reason to celebrate the fact that land was being reclaimed, because I did not agree with *how* it was being taken back, especially the brutal murder of white farmers. I did not want to be "used", to hate on behalf of the rich African political elites. It is very easy for political elites to incite racial violence and give the have-nots false hope that they will be rich after violence, but we have all seen how those stories end in Africa and elsewhere.

Two of our white students had lost a parent through that violent "land reform" program and I sympathized with them. That farmer was known for treating Africans with care and respect. I was scared by how Mrs. Rhodes was provoking me to even think of saying such things. I prefer nonviolent ways of dealing with conflict even though sometimes my emotions try to get the better of me.

Given all that was happening in my life apart from swimming, I was able to handle the situation calmly. My joy as a mother had helped me to remain calm amid storms roiling on many fronts. I could handle the rejection by the father of my children when he chose to cancel our plans to travel to the meet as a family and support our children. What I had not prepared for was a phone call from Sah, his girlfriend, who had the audacity to call me, saying, "Don't travel with children at night; it is dangerous." She wanted me to know *she* was the reason for him not showing up. I cried inside but vowed to stay strong for the children.

Nomalanga and Zanele made history! They were the first of their kind on a formerly all-white Mashonaland Country districts swimming team. So being in Gweru for the gala was a big win for an African mother like me and, of course, for the girls. I asked my daughters if they still wanted to go and they emphatically replied, "*Yes*! With their father (and his car) out of the picture, our travel options had narrowed down to one: hitchhiking.

We stood by the roadside and prayed for safe transport. My four-year-old son, Ntando, was our comic relief. He somehow knew just the right things to say to make us laugh as we waited for someone to stop. Finally, the answer to our prayer for a travel miracle to transport us to Gweru arrived.

It was about 11 p.m. when a gonyet slowed, its air brakes hissing to a stop. I knew it would cost for the ride and I was able to negotiate a good price. The truck had a bed in the back and the driver allowed the girls to sleep there. Happy as I was that we on our way to the meet, I was uneasy about the whole venture. Nevertheless, I put on a brave face in front of the children and encouraged them to sleep. I wanted them to be well rested before the big competition.

It was 3 a.m. when the driver slowed to a stop in downtown Gweru. We had a very early breakfast at Chicken Inn so the girls would have well digested their food before swimming.

When we arrived at the venue around eight o'clock, a sea of private automobiles filled the car park. The majority of the people at the gala were white. I would bet my bottom dollar we were the only family who arrived in the middle of night in a gonyet! Boxes of cold drinks and lots of food was strewn around the grounds. My children and I had neither a cooler nor a stash of food. I was mentally counting my money, praying we would have enough to get back home to Watershed College, the private school in Marondera where I worked as a teacher.

I was always aware that swimming was thought of as a white sport, and an expensive one at that. Nevertheless, when my girls started showing talent, I was determined to support them. I taught them that there is no limit to what they could achieve in life except the ones they put on themselves. At the same time, I made sure they knew I was there for them. Zanele, then nine, was exceptionally gifted, especially so since she had only started swimming earlier in the year.

Za catapulted to fame, going from not knowing how to swim to becoming a pool superstar in a matter of months. Her friend, a white girl I will call Pinky, would not swim after Za started beating her. Their friendship fizzled out. I knew Pinky's older sister was dating a brown-skinned boy at the private school where

I taught. Her parents passionately denounced interracial dating at meetings with school staff, including calling it "disgusting." Since they could not control the love their child had for the boy, they blamed the school. Clearly, the mother was trying to influence her children to shun her brown skinned peers. She succeeded with the little one, but the teenager gave her a hard time.

I spoke with Zanele in 2020, 18 years after those swim competitions. Looking back, she said, "The sad thing is most of the hate was coming from adults. As kids we were just being competitive. No one was racist until they were taught to be so by their parents."

When my children made the All-Africa Games national team, I was told that I would have to sponsor them on my own to travel to Namibia, a distance of nearly 750 miles! They also added conditions that each child needed to be exceptionally accomplished in all four strokes, a change from the initial qualifying criteria of time and nothing else. They had tried to exclude my children by fiddling with time in some of the events, but I had trained as a timekeeper so I could follow every stroke to make sure they were not short changed.

The white people secretly arranged for their swimmers to be sponsored by Colcom, a major Zimbabwean food company then linked to white farmers. Since I didn't have the means to sponsor my girls privately, in the end the girls were not able to go to the All-Africa games. Ironically, I was accused of being a social climber, wanting things that I couldn't afford! They were right; I wanted the best for those of us at the bottom rung of the ladder to be able to climb as high as we could! All I ever wanted was for my children to explore the talents God gave them and be exposed to opportunities. I refused to accept that swimming was a white sport. In my home it was not true. It should not have been true anywhere.

All these years later, my two girls may still hold swimming records at the three primary schools they attended. Lendy Park School wrote a newsletter praising the girls for their outstanding sporting achievements and likened them to Venus and Serena Williams. (That was the closest to the American dream we ever got).

I remember Uncle DX watching Zanele running 400 metres, standing up excited to see her outrun her peers by half the distance. He cheered her on, calling out, "Come on *muzukuru wa sekuru*" "Come on grandchild of Grandpa." He was a proud grandfather. I will never forget that joyful afternoon. Many years later, Uncle DX, now living in the United Kingdom, posted on Facebook, reminiscing from the sporting diaries of his "Olympics material" grandchildren. He wrote about what might have been if they been offered the same support and sponsorship the white athletes received.

Despite our struggles, their experiences contributed to my children becoming strong young adults. Neither expressed regret for not being able to pursue sports because we were not among the "haves." Nomalanga and Zanele are pursuing their passions in clinical psychology and telecoms engineering respectively. They are also working on establishing their own businesses. Their younger brother, Paul Ntando, is also a dolphin who used his swimming abilities to train as a lifeguard in Iqaluit, here in the Canadian arctic. He used his earnings to help pay his aviation training fees. He is now a pilot who dreams of one day owning his own business. Even the sky is not the limit for my children.

They have relationships with people from different walks of

life and multiple cultures. In spite of their experiences, like me, they try to not to make assumptions about people, nor to judge them by the colour of their skin. We have a family agreement that if we ever fall short, we call each other out. As their mother, I feel it is my duty to keep on working on myself and continue to be in dialogue with them. Our aim is to be the best versions of ourselves, paying attention to the lesson life teaches us.

CHAPTER ELEVEN

The Power of a Mother's Teaching

"You must never feel that you are less than anybody else. You must always feel that you are somebody and you must feel that you are as good as anybody else."
—Alberta Christine Williams King, mother of Martin Luther King, Jr.

It was serendipitous to come across this message from the mother of one of the world's most powerful and prominent voices in the fight for racial justice. Its timing was perfect as it came just when I had just finished interviewing my daughter Zanele and completing the previous chapter about her and her sister's swimming experiences. I had delivered more or less the same message to my girls when they had been students at St. Martins, Digglefold and Lendy Park schools where they were learning alongside their white peers. As I sought to emphasize how powerful a mother's teachings are, in terms of influencing a child to be racist or anti-racist, I needed something positive, outside of my personal experience, to reinforce my message.

The wisdom I had been praying for came in the form of a notification from YouTube of an eight and-a-half-minute BBC interview of Martin Luther King, Jr. It was as if it that segment—part of a half-hour interview—had been cut specifically for me. I knew then that I had an invisible guide. No research of my own could have been that precise. Having such strong evidence strengthened me and deepened my self-confidence that I was on the right path. My conviction about the power of a mother's teaching to change the world had been confirmed once again.

When Martin Luther King, Jr. was six, he was upset that his white friends began making excuses for not playing with him. He went to his mother and Mrs. King empowered her son. Like a builder, his divinely guided mother built a strong foundation upon which her son could stand in the fullness of his humanity. It was foundation based on love; a foundation without fear. Of course, that little boy would go on to become the most recognizable face of the US civil rights movement. That was, in part, because his mother's words and teachings were powerful enough to drown the violence that tried to negate the truth.

It is for this reason that I want to share an excerpt from the 1962 BBC interview where MLK shares a part of his childhood story, including the role his mother played in raising him, and how her influence contributed to the man he would become.

BBC: Dr. King, the most unexpected thing to me is for a long time you have been a national leader. You are one of the most influential figures, I suppose, in the United States, and yet you are only 32 years old. Did you have any special training for this kind of leadership when you were growing?

MLK: No, I really didn't. I had no idea that I would be catapulted into a position of leadership in the civil rights struggle in the United States. I went through the discipline of elementary school education, and then high school education, and college and theological training, but never did I realise that I would be in a situation where I would be a leader in what is known now as the civil rights struggle of the United States.

BBC: What sort of home did you have as a child? Was it a strict home for instance?

MLK: Well, I guess it was relatively strict coming up in a minister's home. I faced the discipline that you would face of a fervent religious background. However, I didn't think that it was overly strict to the point that I developed any personality conflict as a result of my early childhood. It was strict, but I think it was strict enough for me develop certain disciplinary principles as I came up.

BBC: When you were still a little boy, before those decisions came along, were you conscious of colour discrimination in your own life?

MLK: Yes, I became conscious of colour discrimination at a relatively early age. I think the first time was when I was about six years old. I had some friends [whose] parents had a store... two white boys and they were my inseparable playmates at the early years of my life and I remember when I was about six something started happening. When I went over to play with them they always made excuses they could not play; they were "busy." And finally, I went to my mother with this problem and she tried to explain to me in the best way she could to a child six years old. This was really the first time that I became aware of the racial difference and of the racial problem. She made it clear to me that this system had a long history dated back to the time of slavery. She tried to explain the meaning of the system of segregation but the things I would always remember is that in the midst of her explanation, she always said to me you must never feel that you are less than anybody else. You must always feel that you are somebody and you must feel that you are as good as anybody else. Of course this came up with me in spite of the fact that I still confronted the system of segregation every day.

BBC: Was that a valid conflict in your life? If you really believed your mother and yet the system around you suggested that this wasn't true. It must have set up some sort of strain? **MLK:** Yes, I think so. As I look back over those early days I did have something of an inner tension. On the one hand, my mother retaught me that I should feel a sense of somebody-ness; on the other hand, I had to go out and face the system which stabbed me in the face every day saying you are less than, you are not equal to. So this was real tension within.

BBC: Out of your own personal experience the only example you have given me so far is one family where the mother didn't have too much care to have you play with her children. What were you really prevented from doing as a child that a white child might have done in your days in Atlanta as a child? **MLK:** It was a pretty strict system of segregation. For instance, I could not use the swimming pool for a long time. I could not go in swimming until the YMCA was built—the Negro YMCA—and they had a swimming pool there. Certainly a Negro child in Atlanta could not go to any public park. I could not go to the so-called white school. We had separate schools and I attended high school in Atlanta—at the only high school for Negroes in the city. And this was a real problem because there were more than two hundred thousand Negroes.

Many of the stores downtown, to take another example, I could not go to a lunch counter to buy a hamburger or a cup of coffee or something like that. I couldn't attend any of the theatres. There were one or two Negro theatres and they were very small but they did not get the main picture. Or, if they got them, they were two years late so that, by and large, that was a very strict system of segregation and there was nothing about racial integration at that time in Atlanta.

Today's systems still promote racial discrimination in overt and covert ways. As mothers, we have power to build or to destroy the future. What we teach our children shapes their behaviour, attitudes, and practice. It starts in our homes, but they take it to school, social clubs, and public spaces, to workplaces. They represent the country.

I wonder what the mother of Martin Luther King, Jr.'s six-year-old friends taught *her* children. How did she explain breaking up the friendship between innocent little boys? We only hear of MLK's sadness. It makes me wonder how the white boys felt. Were they sad, too?

When we abuse our divine capacity to love unconditionally, and teach from a place of fear rather than love, we let our children down. We damage them and they end up hurting each other. We poison their hearts. While they may excel in other aspects of their lives, they will fail in successfully relating with other human beings, people with whom they could be creating beautiful, human experiences. Some even become murderers because of hate. We deny them their full humanity and the ability to live authentically in their purpose.

As individuals, what have we been taught about race? What are our attitudes, behaviours, or practice towards others? What did our mothers teach us about people who do not look like us? Were there teachings based on love or fear?

With "great power comes great responsibility", Spiderman teaches us. As a parent, the question I always ask myself is, "Am I using my power to teach love and compassion, or to teach fear and hate?"

CHAPTER TWELVE

Creating the Future We Want

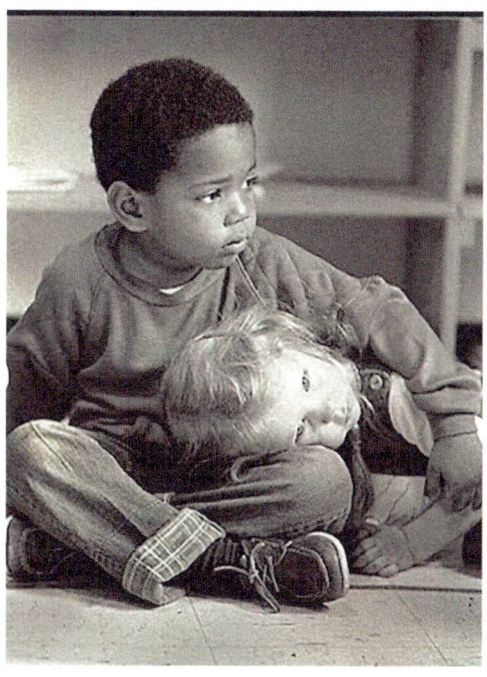

The Age of Innocence
Photo: Marco Mancinelli

In the city of Iqaluit, the capital city of the Canadian territory of Nunavut, there is a strong brotherhood among three innocent little "men", six- and seven-years-old. My six-year-old nephew, Nicho calls his friends Jackson and Hudson, his brothers. No one has told him they are not. That is how he feels about them and no one sat him down to teach him *how* he should feel. I have played with all three of them, fed them, and taught them a few things while at my sister's house.

The fact that Nicho is of African heritage and his friends are Caucasian, is irrelevant to them. "I love my brothers", Nicho says wholeheartedly, not thinking twice about his love for his friends. They reciprocate his love. Never have I heard them talking about race or assigned skin colours. It does not matter to them. What matters is they have each other to play with, fight with, laugh with, *be* with.

When I had an eye operation in 2018, Hudson asked what had happened. I answered, "The doctor cut my eye to remove a cyst." He looked very troubled. "But why did he have to cut you? He is not a nice person." I sighed, "He was helping me, Hudson. He eased my pain. He is a good person." He was still not satisfied. "Okay. Is it very painful?" he asked. "Not that much. I will be fine, Hudson. Thank you for caring," I assured him.

The next few days I stayed home. When I came down to eat, he would check on me, still cursing the doctor for being mean to me. Again, I assured him that the doctor was simply doing his job and that I would be well.

When I removed the bandage, Hudson put on a wide smile and told me that he was really happy to see me well. What melted my heart was the depth of his caring. The beauty of his innocence. His caring heart remains in mine.

Children are angels. They love without boundaries. The beautiful photograph by Marco Mancinelli, "The Age of Innocence", caused quite a stir on social media. "This little girl leaned over to lay her head on the little boy's lap", he explained. "He very gently lifted his arm to receive her." Seeing the photograph touched my heart deeply. It reminded me that if we could all be like children, this world would be a better place.

Nicho goes to Hudson's and Jackson's homes for sleepovers, and they return the visits. They play nonstop. It is so beautiful to witness untainted love. It is inevitable and sad knowing that there will come a time when someone will try to "educate" them about their skin colour." Would it be too much to ask the world, "Please do not corrupt this love? Please do not indoctrinate these children with the poison of racism. They are just Nicho, Hudson, and Jackson to each other—and they are equal beings."

I pray for a time when daycare centers and pre-schools through high schools will work with parents to ensure they teach anti-racism, preserving innocent love, raising the future we want to see. I know that their parents are beautiful people, supporting their children in their desire to enjoy friendships, sharing time with those they love, experiencing brotherhood and sisterhood in a world of possibilities. These children are our future. They are our hope when it comes to making racial equality a reality. More than pray that our racist baggage is not offloaded onto them, I am committed to working for a world where we give them a chance to define their own relationships.

I am not so naïve to assume that only mothers teach children and therefore should be blamed if they grow up to become racist. Print media, television, social media, educational institutions, cultural and social groups also teach children.

How can we learn to cultivate, preserve and protect love, which is threatened by purveyors of hate every day? We must begin with ourselves. We must love ourselves unconditionally and purge all the indoctrination we have absorbed and adopted as truth. We must be conscious and critical, getting to the root of issues. We must educate ourselves and unlearn the lies we have been told. We must be in dialogue with others who are ready to liberate themselves. We must be prepared to learn, unlearn and relearn. We must be prepared to tell the truth, teach the truth, nothing but the truth.

We all have a role to play. Unity in motherhood has a role to play in ensuring a future based on equality. Mothers lay the foundation, but others including, of course, fathers, must also add their bricks to construct healthy human beings. We can indeed raise the future we want to see. It's on us.

CHAPTER THIRTEEN

Know Your Roots: From Africa to America

"I do not greet Africans; they don't wear no shoes, they don't have no houses. They live in the jungle. No, Anna, I do not want to talk to anyone from Africa."

The eight-year-old African American girl's eyes took a tour of my body. Up and down her eyes roamed. I locked gazes with her momentarily until her head moved in a circle the way some Americans roll their heads when emphasizing a point.

Her eyes looked like they were laughing at me. Her lips were slightly pursed. Was it my imagination or was she looking at me as if I was a pile of uncollected garbage? Then she started to walk away, leaving me stunned and heartbroken. She did not want anything to do with "Auntie Franchesca" from Africa.

The little girl did not have to physically pour a bucket of water on me for me to feel drenched in shame and humiliation. I felt the heat of embarrassment rise from my chest to my face. Was I making this scene up or it was really happening? Was an African American looking at me, an African, as less than? I mused. "She is just a child. I have children. Children should not speak like this. Who taught her to look upon me with such disdain? Her parents? Her school? Television? I could only guess. My thoughts were racing.

Meanwhile, my mouth was still agape. If we were home I would have been told to shut my mouth or else a fly would enter. I was not home, for real. I had to catch myself. I closed my mouth while my feet, not bare I swear, but in stylish shoes, played with the soil on which I stood.

I broke the silence. Turning away from the girl, I said to my companion, "Thank you, Anna, for bringing me here. Let's go back," I gently requested. I noticed how red in the face she was, her glistening eyes mirroring the searing pain in my heart. She was like a sister at that moment, so caring and loving. She was a gifted listener, listening with her eyes, ears, and heart. I loved Anna. She meant well, but the visit did not go well.

Anna, my "sister" Training for Change social action trainee, had just introduced me to the little girl. She had been excited about introducing me to people who looked like me, hoping that I would not feel so lost, being in America for the first time. She took me to her neighbourhood. I was one of two Africans from the continent in the Training for Change social action training class of June 2008.

We made our way back to the workshop venue, mostly in reflective silence. "America is the land of the free, the land of dreams." That is what I knew, or thought I knew. Who miseducated this little African American girl? How could she speak such lies with such conviction and confidence, without batting an eye?

One of my main objectives for attending the training was to strengthen emotionally so that I would be a smarter, stronger, more effective change agent. I had already admitted that my emotions often got the better of me; indeed, many had predicted my downfall based on that weakness. Unwittingly, it was an eight-year-old girl whose "training" helped me to become emotionally strong.

Being in multicultural settings opened my mind and my heart in ways I never imagined. I still struggled to understand how those different from me came to be the people they were meant to be, but I certainly learnt to suspend judgment and to listen. Before I came to North America, I had never met lesbians, transgender folks, and other people who identify as queer. I was so naïve. I sat at the same table with these brothers and sisters, broke bread together, conversed together, and did dishes together.

What I learnt was they were human beings just like me, also wanting to be agents of change in their communities. There were very strong people in the training. I realized there were people whom I knew so little about. Still, I understood that there was a direct connection between the struggle for racial equality, and the struggle for gay, transgender, and queer rights. I realized, too, how much I had to learn.

I learnt to be assertive and to speak up when I felt values were being pushed on me and I was being judged as an African. I realized that diversity is beautiful and that we can have different value systems but what is important is listening and respecting each person's rights. And, of course, love must be the guiding principle.

After our evening session, I was happy to return to my temporary home, an apartment in Philadelphia, Pennsylvania. It was the home of a young couple who let me and another participant, from Nepal, stay for free. The young man of the couple was a Jew. He was only the second Jewish person I had ever met. I began to realize then that I needed to educate myself about the centuries of discrimination and marginalization Jews around the world have suffered. Years later, in 2017, I was painfully reminded of that truth when white supremacists marching in Charlottesville, Virginia chanted, "Jews will not replace us!" The connection between racism and anti-Semitism is clear.

I reflected on the image my children had of America and decided to call and tell them of my experiences. "I want you to get my points right. Be proud of who you are as an African. I am happy that you already embrace playing the mbira and that you know where you come from. For that I am grateful. It is important to know our roots and be grounded. Never long to be someone else. Just be you and be content being true to who you are. When I come home I will share more about what I am learning here. Take care and be good to Auntie Lizzie and at school."

I was happy that the children listened attentively, but they were surprised, and disappointed, hearing how that African American child had treated me. I was still sad knowing that while we share the common pain as "Black" people, Africans from the continent experience being looked down upon as "lesser" Black people by some of the descendants of Africans snatched from the continent and sold into slavery. I sighed. The long-held narrative that the world told about Africans had done its job.

For the most part, I was met with sentiments that I suppose were meant as compliments such as, "You speak English very well." I laughed and told them that I was a rural girl and there were many who spoke more eloquently than I, who spoke more like the British.

On the next leg of my US journey, I traveled from Philadelphia to Detroit, Michigan where my "sisters" Jo and Julie lived, and where I had a wonderful experience. I met an African American man who worked at the airport. He ran over to ask if I was from Ghana. I was conspicuous, wearing my large, black and white head wrap and long wrap over skirt and matching top. I smiled and told him, "I am Zimbabwean."

He said, "Joshua Nkomo, he was a great man." (Nkomo was a Zimbabwean revolutionary who served as our country's vice president for nearly a decade). That blew me away. I didn't know people in the US knew good things about Africans, including political icons from my country. He called me a princess, treated me like royalty, carried my bag, and saw me off. I did not get his name, but that experience was special.

At last, the connection I longed for happened. We are one, I thought. The bag he carried was loaded with African organic food and clothing that I brought for my sisters, as well as training materials from my course in community development work. I was filled with gratitude.

It is twelve years later. I hope that the young girl who was so poorly educated about Africans, has grown into a knowledgeable young woman who understands the true history of the continent. I hope she knows that both the descendants of enslaved Africans, and those Africans who have continuously lived in Africa are, in fact, one.

CHAPTER FOURTEEN

Toonik Tyme and The Story of the Rainbow

During the Toonik Tyme Festival, Nunavummiut celebrate for two whole weeks Inuit traditions centered around the return of the sun or spring. Activities include snowmobile races, igloo building, dog team races, craft fairs, sumptuous banquets, and Inuit games. My desire to see people from diverse cultures united and accepted, prompted me to reach out to people who do not look like me to share the beauty of "The Story of The Rainbow". As I shared in my letter to Prime Minister Trudeau, the pain of being treated unjustly in my community drove me to reach out and show people the beauty of love. My mother taught me this as a child before I ever understood why. She never wanted to hit back when people were mean to her; the fierce fighter in me wanted her to.

As I matured and encountered difficult people, I came to realize Mhamha was right. I have found that when we choose love over fear, some people eventually feel our warmth and are drawn to us. Their ice-cold outer shells thaw and they can access the warmth inside of them. It may take time, but I have witnessed this triumph in my life. Love walks hand in hand with peace; we can experience joy even in storms.

With help from Taha Tabish and Nastania Mullin, we secured a slot to perform. That meant we would be able to reach more people of diverse backgrounds and cultures than we would have at if we were sharing say, only at the Catholic church. I was excited because I know that the rainbow story is one of the best tools to jumpstart race and diversity conversations. I felt energy churning within me knowing that we could make a small difference.

How I came to suggest telling "The Story of the Rainbow" has a rich backstory. In 2005, I was unexpectedly selected at a provincial workshop in Limpopo province where Training for Transformation facilitators, Ntombizanele Nyathi, Derick Naidoo, and Priscilla Erasmus were scouting for community change agents throughout Southern Africa. The non-profit organization I worked for, Civic Education Network Trust (CIVNET), which works to empower responsible citizenry in Zimbabwe, had sent a colleague and me to the training. That is where I first performed the story. (I portrayed the color Indigo).

Putting what is known as the CanaDiversity team together was an act of collaboration and cooperation. A group of us quickly built trust and took our parts seriously. Despite not having much time to rehearse, everyone was committed to making a difference in our community. On the day of the performance, each member of the cast dressed as and completely inhabited "their" colour. Green was Stephanie Bernard, a Jamaican. Blue was my blue-eyed friend, Carolyn Sloan from Nova Scotia. Yellow was Sakhile Matshazi a Zimbabwean Canadian girl. Orange was Catherine

Suclan, a Filipina. Purple was Taha Tabish, a Pakistani-Canadian immigrant. Red was Nastania Mullin an Inuk man. Indigo was an Inuk woman, Anna Lambe. Michelle Zakrison, who is Caucasian, dressed in rainbow colours to represent the LGBTQ community. I was the storyteller. The story was written by Anne Hope and Sally Timmel and published in Training for Transformation's own book.

The Story of The Rainbow
A Native Legend

Once upon a time, all the colours in the world started to quarrel. Each claimed that it was the best, the most important, the most useful, the favourite.

Green said, "Clearly I am the most important. I am the sign of life, and of hope.

I was chosen for grass, trees, leaves—without me the animals all would die. Look out over the countryside and you will see that I am in the majority."

Blue interrupted. "You only think about the earth, but consider the sky and the sea. It is water that is the basis of life, drawn up by the clouds from the blue sea. The sky gives space and peace and serenity. Without my peace you would all be nothing but busybodies."

Yellow chuckled. "You are all so serious. I bring laughter, gaiety and warmth into the world. The sun is yellow, the moon is yellow, the stars are yellow. Every time you look at a sunflower the whole world starts to smile. Without me there would be no fun."

Orange started next to blow its own horn. "I am the colour of health and strength. I may be scarce but I am precious, for I serve the inner needs of human life. I carry all the most important vitamins. Think of carrots and pumpkins, oranges, mangoes, and pawpaws. I don't hang around all the time, but when I fill the sky at sunrise or sunset my beauty is so striking that no one gives another thought about any of you."

Red could stand it no longer, shouting, "I am the ruler of you all! Think of blood, life's blood. I am the colour of danger and of bravery. I am willing to fight for cause. I bring fire in the blood. Without me the earth would be empty as the moon. I am the colour of passion and of love, the red rose, poinsettia and poppy."

Purple rose up to its full height, very tall, speaking with great pomp. "I am the colour of royalty and power. Kings, queens, chiefs, and bishops have always chosen me, for I am a sign of authority and wisdom. People do not question me—they listen and obey."

Finally, Indigo spoke. "Think of me. I am the color of silence. You hardly notice me; you all become superficial. I represent thought and reflection, twilight and deep waters. You need me for balance and contrast, for prayer and inner peace."

And so, the colours went on boasting, each convinced that it was the best. Their quarrelling became louder and louder. Suddenly, there was a startling flash of brilliant white lightening! Thunder rolled and boomed. Rain started to pour down relentlessly. The colours all crouched in fear, drawing close to one another for comfort.

Then, Rain spoke. "You foolish colours, fighting among yourselves, each trying to dominate the other! Do you not know that God made you all? Each for a special purpose; each unique and different? She loves you all. Join hands with one another and come with me. God will stretch you across the sky in a great bow of colour, as a reminder that She loves you all the same and that you can live together in peace, a promise that She is with you, a sign of hope for tomorrow."

The audience had been sitting quietly, paying close attention. Now, they burst into sustained applause. After our CanaDiversity team bowed and walked off stage, we made a circle to evaluate how we had done. I cannot forget the spirit that moved among us as we came together. It was as if magic bound us together. An electric current of love coursed through our bodies. No one wanted to let go. There was almost no talking, just a high vibration. The only time I have ever felt that way is when I am with people who know love. I looked into Taha's eyes and Carolyn's eyes, then into the eyes of every person present and felt it. I smiled from inside. It was among us; *love* was among us. Love and acceptance of each other. Our hearts beat as one. How could people who looked so different from one another have such a bond when they barely knew each other? Love is what made it possible.

When I fell asleep that night I wore a wide smile on my face. The sun had come, light had come, hope had not just come, it had returned! I felt joy and fulfilment. I felt a sense of purpose, an alignment with my values. We can love one another in spite of our outer, physical differences.

The Story of the Rainbow reminds us to accept one another without judgement. Genuine collaboration helps us to showcase the best version of ourselves. Too often, we compete instead of cooperating. We think that being the greatest, the smartest, the richest, individually is what's important. Our ego blinds us to the beauty of others. Like the great bow of colour that the rainbow is, together we *all* make up the world; we can all make it a better place. We are richer when we each use our unique gifts to advance the common good.

The pandemic of competition

It is unfortunate that countries compete; their leaders compete; their people compete. Many countries vie to be among the greatest economic and military powers, to feel superior and to dominate the rest. The rainbow story reminds us that we are more powerful when we see our commonality and recognize what is important in life.

One heartbreaking truth is how the coronavirus pandemic also exposed how the most powerful countries—the United States and China—may disagree in ideology and jockey for economic and political superiority; but still agree on one thing—systematically oppressing and minimizing concern for Africans, African

Americans and Afro Caribbeans, Latinx, and other non-whites in the global South more generally. They are seen as unworthy of the same respect as other human beings. There were instances where Africans were beaten and accused of transmitting Covid 19 and spreading it in China. Everyone knew it was a lie; still no world leader publicly condemned such a cruel charge.

Such lies are all too common. A Chinese company created a washing machine advert where a man of African descent "has a pouch of Qioabi cleaning liquid forced into his mouth and is bundled into a washing machine by a smiling woman." When the wash cycle is over he comes out Chinese. The company behind the ad denied it was racist saying, "Any discrimination is in the eye of the viewer," according to a May 28, 2016 *Guardian* article. *Huffington Post* said at the time that the "Qioabi Detergent advertisement might be the most racist TV commercial ever made."

"This is Africa", an exhibit at Wuhan's Hubei Provincial Museum, that presented side by side photographs comparing animals and African people displaying similar expressions, was closed because of its blatant racism, the *New York Times* reported on October 13, 2017. In the US, Chinese shop owners in Black neighbourhoods are notorious for treating Black customers poorly while happily taking their money. Some Chinese employers on the African continent beat up, insult, even shoot employees for simply asking to be paid, or to be able to take their normal days off. One of my daughters back in Zimbabwe, was constantly being berated by a racist male Chinese co-worker. "We are not here to do charity work," he said with scorn. He denied her a reimbursement claim when she used her own fuel to do company work. Instead, he accused her of wanting handouts. She shared that as I taught her to do, she stood up for herself and her voice has led to some changes for all employees. She continues to assert herself in the male-dominated telecoms industry.

ENCA News South Africa shared footage in June 2020 of a Chinese mine owner shooting Zimbabwean men who were simply asking for their salaries to be paid. We have so far to go to achieve equity.

Ignoring both overt and covert racism, it appears that dealing with racism is too uncomfortable for some African elites who instead wine, dine and sign business deals with officials from Chinese companies. It's painful to acknowledge that they allow Chinese people to treat Africans as trash in both Africa and China. After then-US president Donald Trump started saying, "Wuhan virus" and "China virus", many Asians—not just Chinese—became the targets of vicious acts of discrimination, including extreme acts of violence. I was tempted to say, "Now they feel what we have always felt but realized that was not kind and it would not address the problem. So, I empathized and sympathized with them, reminding myself that not all Chinese are like that. I had to guard my heart from indiscriminately hating them all, unfairly including those not involved in beating and ill-treating Africans.

We still have a long way to go to achieve racial equality. My hope is that, like the competing colours of the rainbow, the superpowers will choose to come together and unite in modelling antiracism, bringing human dignity to those treated as lesser beings. Global leaders must begin to unflinchingly face and wholeheartedly commit to channelling the resources required to heal the world of both the recent coronavirus pandemic and the centuries-old racism pandemic.

As I reflect on our CanaDiversity performance, and the love it generated within our cast of storytellers, I also had to boldly face the truth that Canada—my safe place, my home now, known to the world as one of the best countries to live in, a champion for gender equality and multiculturalism—also is battling systemic and unambiguous "anti-Black" racism. I could not articulate Canadian racial inequality better than the excerpt from the article printed below. I came across it as I looked for hard evidence to illustrate the extent of racism in my adopted country. (I did not want to be dismissed, accused of pulling the race and victim cards.)

In the aftermath of the May 25, 2020 police murder of George Floyd in Minneapolis, Minnesota in the US—and the ensuing wave of global protests—many Canadians began to take a closer look at systemic racism in Canada. On June 4, CTV News Canada published an article citing research conducted at Toronto's Yorkville University. Headlined, "Five Charts that Show What Systemic Racism Looks Like in Canada", researchers carefully reviewed the national data; it revealed "the stark racial divide in the country." Here is an excerpt:

"The most recent census data from 2016 shows that Black Canadians face far steeper economic challenges than white Canadians and other racial groups. For example, Black Canadians make significantly less money than non-racialized Canadians regardless of how long their families have lived in Canada. First-generation Black Canadians make an average income of nearly $37,000, compared to an average income of $50,000 for new immigrants who are not members of a visible minority. That wage gap doesn't go away over time. Third-generation Black Canadians make an average income of $32,000, compared with $48,000 for Canadians who aren't a visible minority—a demographic that, due to the way census data is collected, includes Indigenous Canadians, who also experience income disparity."

The Canadian Center for Justice and Community Safety acknowledged that in 2018 Black Canadians were more likely than any other racial group in Canada to be victims of a hate crime, according to data collected by police. Racism is sneaky, especially when embedded in institutions. The acclaimed African American novelist Toni Morrison explains that "…the very serious function of racism is distraction. It keeps you from doing your work. It keeps you explaining, over and over again, your reason for being." Racism inhibits racialized people from living according to their God-given or divine purpose.

Unless those with political power are willing to listen as allies, *and* seek lasting solutions informed and led by those impacted, racial equality will remain a dream. Racism thrives in silence and grows fed by hyperrational arrogance. Racism may present itself differently with African people from the continent and those whose ancestors were snatched from it. We should not be separated; there is no need to feel as if some are better than others. We are the rainbow. We are powerful together as one.

Reflection

I invite you to reflect on The Story of the Rainbow and apply it to your experiences with people who do not look like you. What is *your* story? What is the comparison narrative that the world has taught you about your assigned race in relation to others? How do you feel about the way you identify?

Action

What is the best way to be a part of the solution? For me, it means renewing my commitment to speak truth fearlessly and decisively, drawing on my inner sage. I choose to love, fearlessly and unconditionally, racists and anti-racists alike. It is first and foremost for my own inner peace and happiness and, by extension, for the peace and wellbeing of others. I consciously choose to embrace the power of positivity.

I will not seek to compete for superiority with those different from me; I aim to perceive only one race; as Jane Elliot says, the human race. I will exercise empathy and confront my own racist tendencies and own the conversations I have behind closed doors. I will speak truth, beginning first with myself. I will consciously continue to reduce the darkness inside me and to increase my light. I will be patient and empathetic to those who refuse to acknowledge the darkness in them, those who justify racism and those slowly awakening to their own light.

CANADIVERSITY CAST: Performers of "The Story of the Rainbow." From left: The author, Nastania Mullin, Catherine Suclan, Sakhile Matshazi, Stephanie Bernard, Carolyn Sloan, Taha Tabish, Michele Zakrison
Photo: Ivony Matshazi

CHAPTER FIFTEEN

Had I Known

It is never too late to mend and to heal. We can always do the things we regret not doing because we did not know better. As Maya Angelou said, "When you know better, do better!"

I am determined to be the change I want to see. My commitment to work for change is based on the lessons I have learnt, which I present below as a litany, "Had I Known."

As long as we are still breathing, we all have a chance to do right. The invitation is open for all of us. I share my experience of five decades on this precious planet and offer my story to help foster the uncomfortable conversations we must have if we are to achieve racial equality. How else can we imbue the future with the possibility of being born anew? As both a student and teacher, I understand I am a wounded healer. Where I need more growth and wisdom, I commit to opening my heart graciously, with unconditional love, ready to receive new knowledge, guided by the divine.

Here is my litany:

Had I known that Black is not a skin colour, and that it was created to dehumanize Africans and it is not true that we ever called ourselves "Black" before, I would have created education materials to raise awareness of the dangers of believing in and adapting that racist label.

Had I known that I am an equal human being with equal human rights deserving equal treatment, I would have believed in myself *all* the time and known that my dark skin is beautiful. I would have known that I should concern myself more with the beauty of my heart, following the values of Ubuntu.

Had I known that white supremacy was the reason for my parents' suffering—and that racism is such a pervasive and ugly, divisive, lying monster—I would have started a school to liberate myself and others beginning when I was very young. I would have become a child advocate for economic, political, and social justice.

Had I known that racism is rooted in fear, the fear of loss of control and power over others, fear of exercising power with others, fear of losing privilege (more pay, more opportunities to get into prestigious universities, fear of being downgraded, fear of not mattering and, ultimately, fear of death), I would have advocated for humans to be led by the power of unconditional love and not fear.

Had I known and fully understood the implications of being born in a white supremacist regime, I would have challenged white Zimbabweans to understand their privilege and compelled them to no longer be comfortable with the obscene levels of economic injustice and their entitlement to wealth, no matter how they acquired it.

Had I known that associating whites with "goodness" and Africans with "badness" stems from years of mental enslavement, I would have advised everyone who looks like me to stop self-hatred and investigate why some of us glorify so-called white people and whiteness!

Had I known that religion is the opium of the poor, and is used to keep people docile, I would have liberated myself from mental slavery a long a time ago. I would have reclaimed my culture sooner, knowing that language and culture, 'our first line of defence', grounds us in who we are as a people.

Had I known that not everything described as "Western knowledge and wisdom" is to be passively accepted as the truth, I would have embraced and respected my indigenous African knowledge systems much sooner, honoring my ancestors who never needed missionaries to introduce them to the Divine Spirit (and impose on us *their* definition of God.)

Had I known that "let bygones be bygones" is no way to deal with past trauma and hurt, I would have sought help earlier to confront unresolved childhood trauma and to heal the deep wounds and grief that I was only able to truly begin healing from my thirties and forties, and ever since. Had I known, I would have advocated for trauma healing for entire nations.

Had I known that children's voices matter, and that silence is violence, I would have vocalized my pain and turned it into purpose sooner. I would have advocated much earlier for the widespread teaching and implementation of nonviolence and racial equality.

Had I known that the whole truth, not half-truths, needed to be told, I would have urged *everyone* telling liberation and war stories to tell them honestly, fully, completely.

Had I known that the British system of education was designed to domesticate us, indoctrinate us through manipulation and subtle, coercive persuasion—quieting our potential anger and outrage upon discovering the white supremacist ploy to erase the true history of our people—I would have spoken out sooner. I would have revealed the truth that the British education system in which we were taught to take pride in, is responsible not for open minds but for opiated minds, limited problem-solving capacity and even our hyperrational arrogance.

Had I known, I would have exposed our hyperrational arrogance (which is so similar to some British "heroes", like the racist Cecil John Rhodes.) I would have stopped thirsting for paper validation and instead sought out education that provides practical solutions to life. While some boast of having earned a PhD, individual achievements are almost meaningless in a country seen as a failed state, one that cannot provide evidence demonstrating the value or efficacy of our education. Had I known, I would have advocated for curricula centered around teaching innovation and tackling real life challenges.

Had I known that workplace racism can destroy people's self-esteem and undermine their self-confidence and make them vulnerable to mental illness, I would have both educated myself and exposed how the racial system is so insidious, pervasive, and so entrenched, that even the nicest of people implement their employer's inherently racist agenda. Had I known I would have advocated for comprehensive, ongoing antiracist training for all employees, not just workers, but management, too.

Had I known how to access the tools I'd need to engage with those in authority, I would have used my power to respectfully speak truth to power. Had I known, I would have written my letter to Queen Elizabeth sooner and, I would have sent it.

Had I known that in the 21st century there are leaders making utterances about recolonizing Zimbabwe, I would have educated them about the real impact they were having on Africans, particularly children and their parents. I would have made sure they recognized that colonization is not just a noun; it is also a verb. Colonizing killed millions of Africans. It deprived us of our political, economic and social rights. It was shrewdly implemented through deception, corruption and subjugation. It caused visible and invisible scars, passed on from generation to generation. Had I known, I would have taught emotional intelligence and the beauty of Ubuntu.

Had I known that tackling racial injustice requires more than replacing white leaders with African/African American/African Caribbean leaders, it is about uprooting the architecture of oppression designed to favour whites—and institutionalized over the years through laws and policies in schools, churches, banks, hospitals, cultural groups, and the media—I would have advocated for creating a political education school for the oppressed to understand the system that to this day intentionally devalues them. Until there is new architecture, there will never be a system anywhere that favours equality of African people and other perceived "inferior" races.

Had I known that our own African leaders (mostly male) were using the system created by white supremacists against us—mimicking the oppressor—I would have warned them of the dangers of becoming like their oppressor, desecrating their own values of Ubuntu. I would have advised them not to make a mockery of who we are, turning our Motherland into a laughingstock.

Had I known, I would have advised those leaders that they were playing into the stereotype that Africans cannot lead themselves. Had I known, I would have warned them that, in the words of the Kenyan writer Ngũgĩ wa Thiong'o, "the riches of a few and the poverty of many" is, at its core, unAfrican. In an Africa living in its essential authenticity, we do not leave anyone behind. Had I known, I would have alerted fellow Africans that amassing wealth without regard for equality or sustainability is dangerous for the future.

Had I known that I would be traumatized and retraumatized as an African in North America, I would have equipped myself much earlier with the necessary tools to advocate for racial equality and, in the process, to better guard my mental health.

Had I known that I had a choice to be a saboteur or a sage, I would have worked to develop my sage capacity instead of being seduced by anger to undermine our precious cause.

Had I known that when we operate from fear or other negative emotions, we not only self-sabotage, but we also sabotage others, including the world, I would have started teaching mental fitness to disrupt, intercept, and interrupt this undesirable pattern.

Had I known about authenticity and the value of speaking truth to self earlier, I would have offered to help people who look like me to sit with the uncomfortable truth that so many of us hate ourselves, hate and hurt each other, and that is exactly what racists want us to do so they can continue to keep us down as they seek to destroy us.

Had I known of the power mothers wield as co-creators with the divine, carriers of the sacred womb and the first teachers of children, I would have gathered mothers together sooner to stand in solidarity in our maternal power and demand that a maternal perspective be central to development strategies and overall decision making.

Had I known that there are allies in the LGBTQ+ community whose lives I had been too long ignorant about, I would have much earlier expressed my gratitude for their bravery in standing for all that is just and right. I may not have initially understood their lives, their choices, their liberation struggle, but it is incumbent upon me—and all of us—to educate ourselves, to identify, and to stand with all of our allies.

Had I known that I would convert adversity into the gift of inspiration, I would not have worried about questioning God why I had to go through childhood trauma. I would have seen God's purpose for my life sooner. Now that I know better, I am striving to do better. Now I see the gift and I cannot remain inactive. I am committed to sharing my gifts, my story and my passion as I aspire to change the world by teaching equality, beginning at home. I am convinced that I can change this world; I am not so naïve to think I can do it by myself. That is why I invite you to play your part.

Reflection

What do you wish you had known earlier in your life?
What action(s) are you going to take now?
As the saying goes, just do it!

CHAPTER SIXTEEN

Answering the Call

"Do not fear death, only fear if you have not done what you know you are meant to do."

The author's father,
speaking to her in a dream.

Let the fire in me burn and let the light in me illuminate the world. I am the daughter of fire and light. I am the daughter of I am. I am a weapon of freedom; Francisca I am. Created in the image of I am, fearfully and wonderfully made. Imperfectly perfect in my brown body.

I must answer the call! For me, the call to action for racial equality is not the same as an elective college course. It is *the* core course, required for everyone alive to take. It is a prerequisite for graduating into a world of equality and peace. No semester long "project", it is an action plan humanity must commit to achieving by decade's end.

Race is such a sensitive subject to navigate. I was initially afraid to answer the call; eventually I had no choice. When I was called, I looked in, found my courage, and said, "Yes, I will put my shoulder to the wheel of change, if you lead the way." I know on a deep level that I have not been alone writing this book. My ancestors were with me. My mother and father were with me. The Divine was with me, *is* with me, still.

When something is bigger than us, our egos, we hunger to tune into the Divine and ask for guidance. If we listen deeply, there are always urgent messages to download, to guide us to live the lives we desire—lives of peace, happiness, love, understanding.

Talking to myself and trying to talk myself out of writing, was a real struggle. A voice had whispered in my ear; it was Martin Luther King, Jr. I bristled with resistance. A voice inside replied, "I do not want to watch Martin Luther King videos; I don't want to read his speeches! I am not in his league. Who am I to want to associate myself with such a great man? What could *I* possibly contribute to this world?"

I was wondering why I felt he was beckoning me to sit at his feet and listen to his teachings and understand his dream. This had been going on for more than three weeks.

I wanted to understand why I was feeling the need to carry so much weight on my shoulders; why couldn't I just pay attention to my new life in Canada, making money, helping my children and other loved ones? I was already the author of a book on gender equality; why worry about writing another book, and on race, no less? Why now?

The battle in my mind raged on. I needed to understand why MLK's heart was so big that he could sacrifice so much, taking on the weight of a whole country. After all, he had a loving wife and children he loved; why not just concentrate on them and their wellbeing?

Have you ever heard people ask, "What's in it for you?" when you concern yourself with social justice issues? Or maybe you are one of those who asks that question. What *is* in it for you? I often have been the one being asked whenever I became involved in some social action that was deemed risky. Race was way too big an issue for me. What was in it for Martin Luther King? What was his "why"? Why was he like that? Why are some people like that? Why am *I* feeling like that? That commonality made me curious; I wanted to explore race more closely.

When I shared with my husband that my experience of feeling spiritually drawn to Dr. King was real, his comment was, "MLK confronted race with superior logic. He was a threat to the very core of the system. He was presidential material." The student in me knew that the wisdom I needed to contribute to working for racial justice required the heart and the brain of a King. At the least an open heart and a deeply curious mind. I needed MLK's inspiration. My husband, who does not ask me what's in it for me, encouraged me, but also warned me indirectly. The memory of being taught about Rosa Parks, who ignited the Montgomery bus boycott, came back to me anew.

I can also stand up for what is right, in my own way, in our times, I told myself. I have power that I have yet to tap into as a transformative force. I can use my power, believing in unconditional love and, as a mother, to invite all mothers to stand up in our homes where it's safe, where there will be no arrests, except the arrest of our racially polluted minds that produce hate. We must stand up to teach in our families, schools, and houses of worship. We must stand up in our communities; we must stand up in our own countries to teach our children unconditional love.

I am an African from sub-Saharan Africa, a woman and a mother, with a powerful dream for my children, grandchildren, and great grandchildren to come. My maternal instincts want to protect our children to become their best.

I remembered my own parents. I could feel their resilience in my bones. I remembered visiting the infamous Robben Island prison and the heaviness I felt when I sat in Tata Mandela's cell there. I remembered how I wept upon learning about forgotten hero Robert Sobukwe, the South African political dissident and founder of the Pan Africanist Congress. I remembered Joshua Nkomo and all the other Zimbabwean liberation struggle visionary leaders I admire, including my big brother from my mother's sister, Dr. Kaka Mudambo.

The call grew louder. The call had sounded in so many ways that I could no longer ignore it. It was scary. I resisted waking up when voices kept whispering in my ear, and my head felt as if it was going to explode. My inner dialogue began with not wanting to wake up. I rationalized that I was too tired; then, that I did not want to write a book. I returned to bargaining. I was tired and needed my sleep. Three times I refused to answer the call.

Most of the content in this book came through me in April 2020; much of it while I slept. The words were no longer only a misty whisper; they poured out like a torrential downpour in a tropical rainforest, incessant, traveling so fast that my left ear hurt. They sounded like large hailstones landing inside my ears. It was alarming, traumatizing. My head felt waterlogged. Finally, the discomfort forced me into submission. "Okay, okay… I'll try; I'll write!"

I jumped out of bed, grabbed my diary and a pen from my night table. I held my left temple, covering my ear, which now felt under siege. I wrote out 42 chapter titles, one after another. Afterwards, I felt relieved; the swelling in my head subsided. All of a sudden, I stopped writing. It was done, right? No. My ear kept throbbing; the irritation would not go away. I spoke to my therapist about the pain I felt in my body from carrying within me a book *insisting* on being born. It was as if I was pregnant and I *had* to deliver a book about racial equality. Before long, I went to the hospital where I was treated for a low-grade virus.

I finally gave in to the power of MLK. I was always heartened singing about him in my 2008 "Freedom Song"; it also features other social justice giants like Rosa Parks, Tata Mandela, and Tata Joshua Nkomo. While I hesitated to hear Dr. King's wisdom, I could feel my resistance loosening. Finally, I succumbed. Unconsciously, I fasted the whole day—it must have been part of my spiritual preparation. I sat up in bed, alert and ready. I read, watched, prayed; everything was in silence so I could listen. "I have a dream that my four little children will one day live in a nation where they will not be judged by the color of their skin, but by the content of their character," I heard Dr. King say. I have the same dream for my three children (and for my grandchildren and great grandchildren to come.) I certainly could never compare myself to Dr. King. If I had, I would have had to abandon the idea of writing the book. Now, as then, I am a grateful student sitting at his feet.

Around seven that evening I finally got out of bed. My phone was ringing. A woman I'd recently reconnected with was calling. We had gone to secondary school back in the day and I always think of her as a fierce prayer warrior. She has a sixth sense, intuiting to call me when something big and spiritual is about to happen. I checked in with her, describing my state of anxiety and extreme distress. "I must be crazy spending a whole weekend with Martin Luther King, Jr. and thinking I can make a difference when it comes to racial equality."

She was quiet for a long time. Finally, she said, "You, of all people, do not surprise me that this would be happening. Do what you need to do. Your mission is for the nations. Justice is your ministry. You are bold; you are fearless." I tried to take in her strong words of support. Inside, though, I didn't feel that way. "Really?" I asked myself. "She has no idea how scared I am!" When we hung up I asked myself, "Was Martin Luther King, Jr. not born of a mother?" Yes. My curiosity and line of thought was cheeky and interesting. It was as if I was watching myself from another life.

My racial wound, temporarily—and inadequately—healed by the words "let bygones be bygones" was crying for attention. The "bygones" had failed to go "by"; how could they when the root causes weren't being addressed. There are no shortcuts to healing. Healing my wounds meant squarely facing race issues, asking *why*, again and again, until I could ask no more. It was time to exorcise past demons and, with my eyes wide open, start taking action to realize a better future.

All this had occurred *before* May 25, 2020 (the day George Floyd was murdered), when I had written, "If you are simply checking your white privilege and doing nothing, you are complicit." It was haunting to hear phrases and words I had written weeks earlier, being repeated by real people in the real world. Our wounds were ripped open that day by the brutal nine and a half minutes of murderous insensitivity former police officer Derek

Chauvin inflicted as he pressed his knee on George Floyd's neck. As a mother, it was painful to watch the gift of life ebbing away, the sacred womb being mocked, and my assigned race being brutalized again. Healing meant being willing to be part of the solution. It meant feeling a sense of fulfillment that I was doing what I could, even if I was not a giant like the ones at whose feet I will always sit to learn.

Feeling the love, and convinced about the power of motherhood and unconditional love, I was overcome with a desire to harness that love on behalf of nonviolent social change. My father's message, "Do not fear death, only fear if you have not done what you know you are meant to do," urged me to fulfill my purpose. So I renewed my commitment to working on the book.

It would help me heal through truth telling and to work through my feelings about my childhood, validating everything I felt, including addressing being African in North America.

With the assistance, since 2018, of my therapist, my family, my coaches and sister coaches, I was able to work through most of my childhood traumas. I had space to reconnect with my inner sage who has always been in me; space to evict the victim and hypervigilant warrior in me; space to be vulnerable, and space to be at peace.

My conviction was strong, but it was consolidated when my husband, Sothemba, sent me Nelson Mandela's famous presidential inaugural speech, in which he cited a memorable passage from Marianne Williamson's book: *A Return to Love*. It is a speech I have used to inspire community youth leaders I trained back in Zimbabwe. Now it was time to apply it to myself.

"Our deepest fear is not that we are inadequate. Our deepest fear is that we are powerful beyond measure. It is our light, not our darkness that most frightens us. We ask ourselves, 'Who am I to be brilliant, gorgeous, talented, fabulous?' Actually, who are you not to be? You are a child of God. Your playing small does not serve the world. There is nothing enlightened about shrinking so that other people won't feel insecure around you. We are all meant to shine, as children do. We were born to make manifest the glory of God that is within us. It's not just in some of us; it's in everyone. And as we let our own light shine, we unconsciously give other people permission to do the same. As we are liberated from our own fear, our presence automatically liberates others."

We are all created equally. We are all meant to shine. We should answer the call to action. For my part, I have fully surrendered and answered the call as best as I can. In the months and years ahead, I expect to find myself speaking to audiences interested in exploring social justice dialogue and questions. I am ready to serve. I will likely write more books; I hope they will reflect a legacy of equality, love, and freedom—to the extent that I am able. If I were to die today, I would smile and say, "I have done one of the scariest things I know I was meant to do." *My grandchildren and great grandchildren will not spit on my grave!*

Knowing that *you* are powerful beyond measure, and that *you* have a choice to answer the call, are you listening? Are you ready to answer?

CHAPTER SEVENTEEN

United Nations Sustainable Development Goals

A Call to Action for Racial Equality from Home to Globe

In 2015, the United Nations General Assembly established Sustainable Development Goals (SDG), 17 interlinked global goals designed as a universal call to action to end poverty, protect the planet, and ensure that all people enjoy peace and prosperity. It is hoped these SDGs will be achieved by the year 2030.

I am fearless. I am a game changer, a legacy builder. I am my own liberator. I am a mother, a mother trying to do her best. I have raised the future and continue to do so. I am a future ancestor! Does this sound like you, too—someone working for a sustainable future?

To me, "sustainable development" means using resources responsibly, conservatively, in order to ensure the future is liveable and peaceful for our children, grandchildren, great grandchildren, and all future generations. Of course, there can be no sustainable development without paying close attention to racial equality. In that context, a critically important question must be asked: How can development be sustainable for *all* people?

In my 2019 book, *Mother Behold Thy Son: One Woman's Journey to Dismantle Patriarchy and Live a Life of Equality, Love and Freedom*, I shared what I think of as my gender inequality story. It was anchored in a call to action to achieve the SDG 5 calling for gender equality. I brought the goal into the home by asking individuals and families to take action to advance gender equality. Now, in the absence of similar clear and specific goals for racial equality, I am left asking why the United Nations did not design a dedicated sustainability goal to address the most pervasive of all inequalities—racial inequality? Doesn't racial inequality also deserve concrete deliverables that can be measured and monitored over time to ensure that there will be peace around the world?

I was taught that in the context of people's actual lives, development means meeting human beings' fundamental needs which are, in fact, their fundamental *rights*. I was lucky I learnt about SDGs as part of my education; I've always wondered why they are not taught to everyone? In my view, for anyone hoping to make a difference in the world, awareness of sustainable development goals is crucial. Truth is, *all* of our individual, family, community, and country actions contribute to making life better for everyone. It would be great to know the individual and collective impact we are having as we each seek to live fully, according to our purposes.

The 17 sustainability goals are tied to each development problem to be solved. While SDG 10 tries to embrace race, it is bundled in with other inequalities, unlike the stand-alone, more prominently addressed goals, such as gender equality. The same focus and attention must be given to race. It must also be a stand-alone goal with specific deliverables, including its own budget to help ensure its success.

As a woman, I regularly experience the double jeopardy of gender and racial inequality. While I, of course, also acknowledge other minorities, race is the universal injustice that cuts across all of humanity and it disproportionately impacts Africans and African descendants.

In February 2020, I started writing an 18th SDG goal addressing racial equality. It is my dream that the UN will establish it as an independent goal. I started thinking about the need for it when Black history month began. I do not think that the history of my people should be remembered in only one out of twelve months. It should be acknowledged *every* month. The term "Black history" means many things including, in my mind, being the history of wealthy countries whose wealth was largely achieved through the sweat and blood of Africans and other minorities. That reality should be at the center of the curriculum offered by every educational institution so the world will know the truth about our lives. Acknowledging that truth is essential if we hope to realize peace and development for all.

The world has unashamedly and unflinchingly punished those of us gifted with melanin by assigning us to the bottom rung of the race ladder. This happened despite so much of the world's cultures having been sustained by our sweat and blood. They exploited our resources, stole our identity, salted our wounds and drew tears of blood. They did all this while simultaneously seeking to wash away our sweetness and humanity and fattening their coffers as they became among the wealthiest of nations.

Many global institutions were founded—and are led—by the

privileged, and are based on principles conceived by wealthy nations. To date, development has been defined by them and is for their benefit. Surely, if development was defined by people who look like me, no nation would ever allow the commonplace—and normalized—decimation of Africans and Afro-descendants. Now is the time for the world to make things right, beginning at the root.

It is high time to speak the truth: unless the unjust system upon which our development is premised is reformed—and racial equality is given prominence and priority as a stand-alone goal—no true development and peace will be achieved by 2030. Unless institutions acknowledge that systemic racism and white privilege is real, there will be no peace by 2030. Unless we all commit to being the change we want to see by acknowledging, owning, and transforming our part in perpetuating the status quo, there will be no peace by 2030. Unless we accept the undeniable truth that we are one human race and remove all blame, guilt, shame—and commit to healing ourselves and to never again allowing a system of dominants and subordinates, top rung of the ladder and bottom rung—there will be no peace by 2030. We all have a role to play to transform our societies.

As a world citizen, and a mother concerned for the wellbeing and future of all children, I humbly implore leaders to adopt a maternal lens to development goals, and to help raise our children to be free from hating and killing each other, and themselves. I implore leaders to understand the bond a mother has to her child, the connection deeper and longer than the umbilical cord. I implore humanity to go back to respecting the womb, the carrier of sacred life. I am pleading with all leaders to commit to nonviolence and to refrain from hate, force, and fear to solve problems.

Please know if you don't, your actions will come back to haunt mothers, the givers of life. Ubuntu has taught me that human life is more important than acquiring wealth; it's more precious than making and spending money.

I implore mothers to unite and speak with one voice. I implore mothers to demand a place at every decision-making table, and to remind the decision-makers that life is sacred, and decisions must be made with the aim of saving every life and giving all children the opportunity to fulfill their dreams. Always remember, without mothers there would be no human beings.

We have to begin at the individual level, with ourselves. I have been doing the work of forgiving myself, and others, and seeing each child as another mother's child and, by extension, *my* child. My power as a mother has helped me influence how my children treat other human beings. I taught them gender equality in my home and I taught them racial equality in my home. They all at some point attended schools with Caucasian classmates and made friends across cultures so I had to empower them.

With the submission of my proposal are actions we all can begin at home while we await global leaders taking action.

A Call for a New UN Sustainable Development Goal

Achieve Racial Equality and Empower All People

GOAL: **Racial equality.** Ending all racial discrimination is not only a basic human right; it is crucial for a sustainable future. It is clear that certain races are being systematically deprived of opportunities to achieve economic growth and development. Further, we must abolish all laws and systems that perpetuate racial injustice to bring equality for all races. It is crucial to pay attention to the disproportionate racism directed towards Africans and Afro-descendants, and to go to the root of systemic racism.

Racial Equality Targets

1. End all forms of discrimination against Africans, Afro-descendants and other Indigenous peoples and minorities. The disproportionate racism towards Africans and Afro-descendants must be acknowledged.
2. Eliminate all forms of racial violence against all peoples in the public and private spheres, including: ending all harmful practice, such as: shooting to kill African peoples, Asians and Indigenous peoples, lynching, and intra-racial hate and violence.
3. Recognize and equally value work done by Africans and African Americans, Latinx, and Native peoples as a way to begin to correct current and past economic injustices.
4. Undertake reforms to give all racially oppressed people equal rights to economic resources, as well as access to ownership and control over land and other forms of property taken from them. Also, offer them comprehensive financial services and reparations.
5. Initiate the process of reconciliation in the form of both written and spoken apologies that acknowledge all past injustices and include concrete commitments to expeditiously correct past wrongs and begin the process of reparations.
6. Enhance the use of technologies, in particular information and communications technology, to promote the empowerment and protection of all racially oppressed people.

7. Adopt and strengthen policies and enforceable legislation to promote racial equality and the empowerment of all cultures at all levels through relevant quality education.

These targets are suggestions based on SDG 5, gender equality. I invite you to use these targets as a guide to help in heeding any and all calls to action. The targets help us measure our progress as individuals, families, communities, organizations, countries, continents—the whole world. Feel free to add more targets as you reflect on your reality and take laser focused, clearheaded, and decisive action to achieve racial equality. The time for action is now!

Call To Action

We must acknowledge the work that is already being done. Begin by asking the question: What are you already doing to meet the targets above? Celebrate your achievements! They say what gets celebrated gets repeated. Below are the calls to action.

Because it should be the world's most powerful organization, we urge the United Nations to play a significant role in taking on racial inequality so that sustainable development can be a reality for all peoples and all nations by 2030.

United Nations

Call to Action #1

I call upon the United Nations to adopt the idea of a separate Sustainability Development Goal for Race if the world is to experience true development and peace by 2030. Commit financial resources to advancing anti-racist legislation, policies, and implementing programs based on the proposed targets.

Call to Action #2
A) I call upon the United Nations to reform the language that the world imposed on Africans and continues to use to perpetuate racial injustice and, consequently, inequality. Use accurate, common, and universally applicable terms and descriptors of people. For example, identify people by geography and cease using the binary race terms "black" or "white,"(which are known to be invented by the stroke of a pen and therefore a lie). We already use the terms Asians, Indians, Africans, Americans, etc.

B) Eliminate the imposition of race labels on forms by governments, immigration offices, financial institutions, hospitals, and all other organizations that collect personal data and leave no choice for those who do not want to identify as Black or white.

C) Eliminate the terms "wealthy nations" and "poor nations" when discussing development. Such terminology promotes narratives based on the power differential created from an unjust system where 'wealthy nations' have benefited from exploiting Africans and their resources. Africans and other nations are regarded from a deficit perspective that reinforces the world treating them poorly and justifying their actions.

Call to Action #3
I call upon the United Nations to employ a maternal lens in examining development, and invite mothers and grandmothers (birth,

earth and by nurture), to a seat at the global decision-making table (as a special council). A woman's presence will ensure that respect for the sanctity of life is taken seriously. As womb bearers, women have the strongest interpersonal connections with their children (no matter how old), so they have deeper appreciation for the value or life.

Call to Action #4
I call upon the United Nations to create global racial healing campaigns and programs based on the proposed new SDG Racial Equality; model it after Gender Equality SDG5. As such, it should similarly be promoted through continuous engagement, world conferences, and actions by all institutions and systems involved.

Call to Action #5
I call upon the United Nations to ensure that SDG4 on quality education includes anti-racist education in school curricula to promote equality for all. (Transformative pedagogies such as Jane Elliot's are a must).

Call to Action #6
I call upon the United Nations to promote peaceful conflict resolution among nations so that individuals and families never glorify violence as a conflict resolution tool.

Call to Action #7
I call upon the United Nations to decolonize decision-making bodies based on power and wealth and which exclude less developed countries.

Canadian Government

Note: *As I describe these calls to action, I acknowledge how grateful I am to call Canada home. I do not, and will not take the safety, opportunities, and hospitality this country offers for granted. I recognize that because of my privilege of being abroad, my life is easier than many others back home and elsewhere. So this is a humble submission, informed by the fact that no matter who I am or where I am, I should feel worthy and know without a doubt that I am an equal human being.*

Call to Action #1
I call upon the federal government to support the call to the United Nations to establish a separate SDG for racial equality, including clear deliverables for racial equality. Canada has already set a global example with gender equality; doing the same for racial equality would be true to its values.

Call to Action #2
I call upon the federal government to formally consult with Africans and Afro descendants to learn what they need to experience racial justice and equality in Canada.

Call to Action # 3
I call upon the federal government to eliminate the use of language that perpetuates the race binary, and invite legislators to use language that is inclusive, truthful, sensitive, safe, and free from racial prejudice. I call upon the federal government to end the race binary by instructing those who collect demographic information to remove any references to "black" and "white" in federal, provincial and territorial documents. (It may be necessary first to establish a language commission to ensure language is agreed upon).

Call to Action #4
I call upon the federal government to support racial trauma healing initiatives, programs and policies so that the multicultural Canadian population is unified in its diversity.

Call to Action #5
I call upon the federal government to introduce racial equity programs that remove barriers and aim to bring racially disadvantaged groups on par with Caucasians. Census records reveal that African people are earning $32,000; for whites the figure is $48,000. First, bridge the gap; then offer grants—not loans. Loans increase debt and in many instances could undermine efforts to achieve equality for people who may lack the confidence and self-esteem to, for example, start a business. Provide programs that advance their empowerment.

Call to Action #6
I call upon the federal government to finance the training of police officers to treat Africans and Afro descendants equally, as the Iqaluit Royal Canadian Mounted Police is striving to do.

Call to Action #7
I call upon the federal government to correct historical economic injustices by making companies built on a foundation of the sweat and blood of African and Indigenous people reimburse those communities for the free slave labour and cheap labour they received which is largely responsible for their becoming wealthy.

Call to Action #8
I call upon the federal government to respect immigrants' education by making integration easier and the job market more equitable.

Call to Action #9
I call upon the federal government to uphold SDG4 (quality education) by including African peoples' history and literature in school curricula.

Call to Action for African Leaders

I make this call to action knowing that I am an African child raised to respect my elders and to love my community, and to act in ways that make my people proud. I speak to the current leaders, most of whom are my father's and mother's age, as their child who wishes to see racial justice in the world and true freedom for all Africans.

Call to Action #1
I call upon African Leaders to adopt the idea of a racial equality sustainable development goal as proposed and to move to advance the agenda globally.

Call to Action #2
I call upon African leaders to return to the African values of Ubuntu—"I am because you are"—and to lead and protect their own people.

Call to Action #3
I call upon African leaders to liberate the Motherland by recognizing the truth that Africa is the provider of crucially important resources to the world. Further, they should emphasize that Africa is not poor, and it should lead the continent in the pursuit of sustainable development and peace.

Call to Action #4
I call upon Africa leaders to create education systems that liberate Africans from mental enslavement and that promote innovation and critical consciousness.

Call to Action # 5
I call upon African leaders to denounce and prosecute false prophets, and to refrain from using churches to opiate Africans (as the colonizers did.)

Call to Action # 6
I call upon African leaders to initiate trauma healing for all former colonies and to deal with self-hate and xenophobia on the continent.

Call to Action # 7
I call upon African leaders to design nonviolent, racially just, land reform programs that respect the land of our ancestors and reflect the initial reasons for engaging in armed struggle: to seek economic, political and social freedom for all African people. Put African peoples' lives and wellbeing first—before money—and treat all human beings equally and justly no matter which side of history they are on.

Call to Action for Employers

Call to Action #1
I call upon employers to provide antiracist and cultural competency training for all employees so that the workplace is safe and fulfilling to work in.

Call to action #2

I call upon employers to be authentic regarding endorsing diversity and inclusion initiatives and to learn more about multiculturalism and how to achieve racial equality.

Call to Action #3

I call upon employers to provide counselling and trauma/healing support for employees, and to create programs for those who need ongoing support (As one of my former employers has done).

Call to Action #4

I call upon employers to immediately ensure that employees are paid equally, no matter who they are and where they come from.

Community

Call to Action #1

I call upon communities to have the difficult conversations and to do so respectfully, ensuring that during all dialogues, a safe space is created. Clearly spell out the rules of engagement which I borrowed from counselling and group facilitation: no judgement, no repercussions, unconditional love, unconditional positive regard. The Story of the Rainbow is available to jumpstart difficult dialogues in a creative and engaging manner.

Call to Action #2

I call upon communities to confront the issue of self-hate and violence in communities by tackling root causes and refusing to perpetuate victimhood.

Call to Action # 3

I call upon communities to initiate community-driven healing processes, making sure to involve children and youth.

Family

Call to Action # 1

I call upon parents to schedule time for weekly family dialogues about your multiple identities—including race—and to discuss how you are contributing to racial equality (using the proposed targets as well as your own). For consistency and to create a family tradition, make it on the same day each week.

Call to Action #2

I call upon parents to teach children about their rights and responsibilities, using as a guide the United Nations' Convention on The Rights of the Child. Article 2 states: "All children have these rights, no matter who they are, where they live, what their parents do, what language they speak, what their religion is, whether they are girl or boy, or nonbinary, what their culture is, and whether they are rich or poor. No child should be treated unfairly for *any* reason." Every child matters. Every child is created for a special and unique purpose.

Call to Action #3

I call upon families to use technology in general, and communications technology in particular, to promote empowerment of your family. Use social media, i.e. YouTube, Tik Tok, Facebook, Instagram, Twitter to take action against racism.

Educators

Call To Action #1
I call upon educators to teach truth and offer relevant education that helps students to solve real challenges that life presents.

Call to Action #2
I call upon educators to teach empathy and compassion.
And use transformational pedagogy, similar to the "Blue and Brown Eyed" experiment Jane Elliot devised.

Individuals

Call to Action # 1
Wheel of Race Relations

I invite you to draw a circle and divide it up into at least five parts, each representing people that do not look like you. Make sure to include Africans, Afro descendants and Indigenous peoples, Latinx, and Asians. Be specific. Label each part with the assigned racial label. To determine whether you are racist or nonracist, rate yourself from a scale of 1 to 10: 1 means "I am nonracist" and 10 meaning "I am very racist." Be brutally honest. Make sure you can justify your score to yourself. Think about your scores and what they represent, focusing on: your attitude, behaviour, and practice towards each group of people you have identified. Shade each section with different colours to create a visual of your race relationships. (If you are not shading at all, you are suggesting that you are 100 percent anti-racist!)

If you feel overwhelmed, gently remind yourself of the wisdom of being non-judgmental of yourself, others, and of life.

We are not avoiding difficult work; we are confronting it with "blameless discernment", as Shirzad Chamine, author of *Positive Intelligence*, says.

As you honestly review your scores, remember to be gentle and be compassionate with yourself. We are all products of our socialization. We were programmed to think, act and feel the way we do. Now, fortunately, we are beginning to consciously examine that programming and choose what is humane and discarding what is not. In this exercise, as in life, it is important to understand that there is no place for guilt and shame, only unconditional love of self. We all have our good side and our bad side. We all were born with innate goodness. Remember to access it.

After looking at how you rate your relations with people that do not look like you, you can then determine what next steps you need to take.

Call to Action # 2
Invitation to use positive intelligence, the power of the sage to transform race relations

1. **Build Your Empathy Muscle**
   Begin with yourself. Love yourself unconditionally. Forgive yourself for the racist tendencies you were born into or taught . Look at everyone you encounter and recognize their humanity and worthiness to be loved unconditionally. The story of a Muslim mother who forgives her son's murderer is a powerful example of empathy. As human beings, we have the capacity to love that much; still, it's a choice we have to consciously work to achieve.

2. **Choose Curiosity, Not Assumptions**
   To avoid offending and hurting others, encourage curiosity over making assumptions. "I am curious. How can I support you at this time?" With this approach, you will get to hear what matters most to the person with whom you are having a conversation.

3. **Be Innovative, Positive, and Creative**
   Think of new ways of dealing with race relations to avoid unnecessary conflict. Find the positive aspects and truth in what the person you are having a conversation with is saying. Affirm them, then, without dismissing their story, respectfully make your contribution non-confrontationally.

4. **Purpose**
   Take time to think about your purpose and what it is you were created to do; zero in on race and reflect. Recognize that each human being, no matter who they are or where they come from, are on this earth for a special purpose.

5. **Action**
   When we are accessing our inner sage—our state of wisdom—our actions result in positive outcomes. When marching for causes and advocating for racial justice, be clear-headed, laser focused, and decisive about the actions you are taking to ensure a positive outcome. Love not fear must lead your action.

6. **Always have a sage perspective**
   Coach Shirzad taught me that when you adopt a sage perspective, you are able to see the gifts and opportunities

in any circumstance or outcome. Your life is that of ease and flow. You evict yourself from "Victim Street" and accept that in whatever your circumstances, there are gifts and opportunities no matter which side of history you are on. Such self-work in this call to action requires one to have practical tools to *be* in—to access—their sage. Ibram Kendi reminds us that "like fighting an addiction, being an antiracist requires persistent self-awareness, constant self-criticism, and regular self-examination." In our anti-racist mental fitness courses at www.franciscamandeya.com) We go deeper—in terms of the level of self-work. We provide a science-based operating system, and a strong accountability system which is a critical success factor in any human endeavour. We are aware the insight from reading books or attending courses alone is not enough to bring about lasting change! I hope you are curious and will connect with me and we get to teach and learn from one another.

Call to Action #3
Invitation to Use Language that Promotes Racial Equality.

1. Label by Skin Colour: If you agree that "black" or "white" is a lie and therefore not your skin colour but a political construct, start using descriptors that are accurate for you. For example, I use African instead of Black.
2. Use active, empowering language. Notice the difference in these two sentences: "Africans were colonized and became slaves" *vs.* "The British colonized Africans, forcing them into slavery." Note the difference between passive

and active voice. Shift from victimhood to resilient victor and place responsibility for slavery, colonization or oppression where it belongs.

Call to Action #4
Read Your Reality and Write Your Own History

What is your story? What is your belief system? What does it teach you about love and respect for the sanctity of life?

- Are you a descendant of the enslaved who were colonized? If so, how are you using your history to liberate yourself and write a new history? (If you are an ally and not a descendant of the enslaved, what are you doing to liberate yourself?)
- Are you racially oppressed? If so, how are you ensuring that you use your story to liberate yourself and write a new history?
- Are you a descendant of slave owners and colonizers? If so, what are you doing to acknowledge your history—recognizing it is a history you did not choose? What are you doing to liberate yourself from that history?
- Are you from a family where you have African as well as Caucasian blood or from many cultures? If so what are you doing to be at peace ?
- Are you from a country that overtly mistreats racial minorities and does not call out and decisively act to prevent injustice? If so, what are you doing to contribute to racial equality? What history are you writing by your actions? Remember, silence is violence. We cannot pretend this truth does not exist. To do so is criminal to our future.

- Just as I have told my story, you can also tell yours. Connect with me if you know you want to tell your story but may not know how to begin and tell it safely.

Next Steps:
Based on the suggested racial equality targets, calls to action, and your opinion, what are your first steps? Use the diagram below to map your actions.

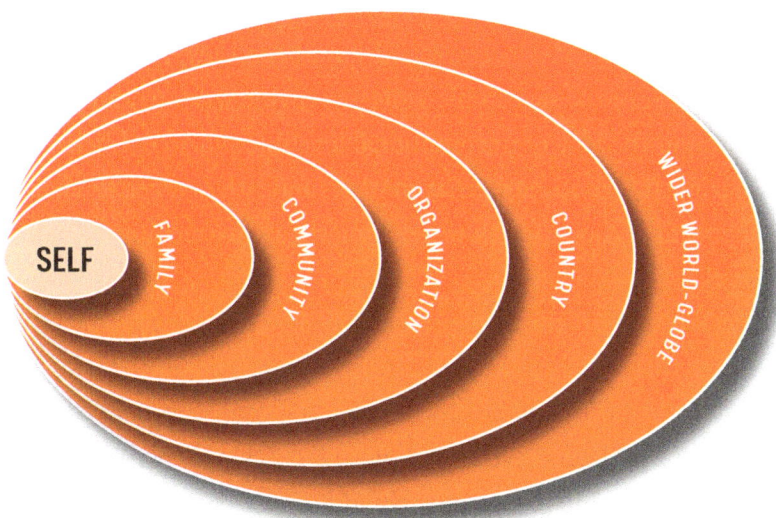

In my life, I have learnt about different types of power: the power of knowledge, the power of force, the power of position, the power of the sage, the power of religion, the power of love, the power of unconditional love. We all have more than one power. What powers do you possess, and for what do you use them? Which of your multiple identities give you the most influence to change the world?

I invite you to stand in your full power and make a difference. Each one of us has their own unique power! Real world change will happen when we all work on changing ourselves. I am continuously learning and doing self-work when I do my mental fitness training and transformational coaching work. I have to practice what I teach. I am not perfect but I am laser-focused on my goal. As a mother, the power of unconditional love is what motivates me the most to work for the future I long to see. Like all mothers who have a special bond with their children, I have influenced my children's behaviour starting when they were in my womb up to this day. I am aware that when it comes to parenting, control is illusive, but influence is real. I have been learning more about the power of the sage, which gives us divine wisdom and teaches us to put the idea of unconditional love into practice. I believe in sharing the good news that mothers have the power to change the world if they commit to teaching their children unconditional love!

We tend to think the world will be changed by others; we forget that we are *all* meant to play a role. *We* are our own liberators. We can liberate our minds. As a counsellor and coach, I remind you that everything we need for change is within us. Our hearts are within us and our thoughts are ours; our reactions and responses are up to us, we can control them. We only have to choose our path. It is either unconditional love or fear. I choose unconditional love. Join me.

Final Reflections

Being an African woman and an immigrant, I have learnt truths about myself, my motherland, and North America. These truths were not easy to acknowledge, process and share. The triple impact of colonization, white supremacy, and systemic racism awakened in me a deep awareness of why I think, feel and act the way I do. I confronted demons as tall as Mount Kilimanjaro. I climbed on top of them and shouted! I overcame! My story was lodged deep inside my body and now I have offloaded an enormous weight; one I'd been carrying for decades. I hope when you tell your truths you will also experience release and healing. I also hope you will understand why I had to be vulnerable and brutally honest; showing you my human imperfection.

My dream is that we all unite—from the home and the village, the town and the city, the province and the state, the country and the globe—and agree to follow only one guiding principle: unconditional love. I am willing to be of service to those who, like me, believe that the power of unconditional love will cure the world of hate. It is not always easy to heed the call. We fear our own light. We fear being called imposters. We fear rejection; we fear going against society, including those in positions of power, our loved ones, and those who are not kind to the oppressed.

Fear is only driven out by love. Love of self, love of others, love of the divine and love for action. Because of our different lived experiences, our stories are different. However, my story is meant for anyone; at its core, it is *your* story, too. It journeys from the oppressed to the oppressor; the one whose ancestors were enslaved, and those who were slave owners and those neither black nor white. My story is not only medicine for me, it is also for you; it is for anyone ready to open her eyes, ears, and heart to the truth. It is for anyone who wishes to work for racial equality. It is for those courageous enough to realize that living in victimhood—where we experience highs from shaming, blaming and guilt-tripping others—is neither going to make racial inequality, or our pain, go away. It is for those who, through the power of community and a commitment to advancing systemic change—and who are prepared to acknowledge, own and transform the status quo—that change will come.

Francisca, my Catholic name, means weapon of freedom and Ndaiziweyi my indigenous name, means Had I known? I have a weapon to ensure my freedom, an axe used during a war fought centuries ago; now an axe used to cut all ties of mind control—from victimhood to hypervigilance—freeing my sacred mind to be open to loving life, no matter what curveballs life throws at me. My axe is not meant to harm other human beings with its sharpness, no matter who they are or where they come from, or what their ancestors have done. My axe is strictly used to clear away the stumps in the path on my way to freedom, our freedom. I have converted my loaded Indigenous name which expresses regret, disappointment, and pain into an empowering name. I have no regrets for all my circumstances. There are gifts in our circumstances.

I am grateful to you, dear reader, for taking this journey with me, from reading stories of the joys and sorrows of my childhood, to the fiery self-examination I undertook on the road to the fullness of my womanhood. Of course, at its heart, the book features stories of race, racism, and the road to freedom—mine, and yours. From the private sphere to the public sphere, I sought to reveal my multiple identities through the experiences that make me the woman I am today. I am a victor of my life, not a victim of my circumstances.

As I end this book, I am curious about *you* and *your* experience of the book. What is the most significant thing you learnt from my story? What fears did you have, if any? And what fears do you no longer have ? If you still fear, what is the deepest one? Rosa

Parks taught me that "when one's mind is made up, this diminishes fear; knowing what must be done does away with fear." I hope you make up your mind and get to know what must be done.

What are you excited and nervous to continue to explore? How do you see yourself in your own environment? Where are you *now*, after reading this book—both spiritually and physically? Are you in a rural or urban area; a big city or small town? Are you in a place of expansion or contraction? Are you in Canada or the United States? Are you in Asia or Australia? Maybe you are in South America, or somewhere on the glorious African continent? Where is your heart living now?

I would love to hear from you. Join me on my website www.franciscamandeya.com or if you are a mother, on www.mothersunited.ca. I have created safe spaces for us to continue the work on ourselves, our families, communities, organizations, and countries. Remember, unconditional love is the only cure for racism; it is our only hope for the future. Take care.